Ghosts

I HAVE TALKED WITH

By

HENRY C. McCOMAS

Department of Psychology, Johns Hopkins University

BALTIMORE
THE WILLIAMS & WILKINS COMPANY
1935

COMPOSED AND PRINTED AT THE
WAVERLY PRESS, INC.
FOR
THE WILLIAMS & WILKINS COMPANY
BALTIMORE, MD., U. S. A.

To
the sweetheart of my boyhood
the wife of many years

FOREWORD

To PUBLISH another book on spiritualism, while the spruce forests are being so quickly depleted to make the pages of important works, would seem to be an economic crime. No one who believes in spiritualism ever changes his opinion by reading arguments against it. Few who do not believe are won over by anything they read. What possible justification can there be for a book of this sort? None, so far as the author can see. It is perpetrated at the instigation of a number of insistent friends. It was their belief that the point of view of a scientist who had tried seriously to learn something about modern spiritualism would prove of value to many people who are interested but are neither believers nor unbelievers. I hope that they are right.

THE AUTHOR.

Baltimore, Md.
September, 1935.

CONTENTS

CHAPTER I

WHY THE PSYCHOLOGIST?

WHEN a psychologist is introduced to his fellow citizens anywhere, except beneath the classical shades of the university, he has a feeling of embarrassment. The reason for this is quite obvious. Psychology is the most over-advertised subject in the world. The opinion seems to have gone abroad that the psychologist is a sort of superman. No one knows better than the psychologist how bad a mistake that is. Every summer when I go on vacation I instruct the family to keep the secret that I have earned a precarious livelihood teaching psychology for a number of years. Often the secret leaks out, *via* the mother-in-law. Then such embarrassing incidents as these have appeared.

A very charming young lady with very large hazel eyes jockeyed me into a corner of the hotel porch. There the following conversation ensued:

"Doctor, will you do me a favor?"

"Of course, yes, anything you ask."

"Well, you know, I sing a great deal and I'm haunted with an ambition to go into grand opera. If I do, I shall have to leave my husband and little Paul. So I want to ask you to hypnotize me and rid my mind of this torment."

1

All the while she kept looking at me with those great hazel eyes, so I replied, "Madam, if this keeps up one moment longer, someone will be hypnotized but it won't be you."

Hardly had I recovered from this encounter when a man with whom I had been playing billiards and swimming slapped me on the shoulder and exclaimed, "Mac, I hear that you are one of those—one of these—err—err, (sigh) ser—"

"Do you mean a psychologist?"

"Yes, that's it! They tell me you're one of those."

I admitted it.

"Well, old man, will you do me a favor?" said he, with a very earnest expression in his eyes.

"No" I said, "what is it?"

"A few days ago I lost my stick pin. I thought a great deal of that pin. I certainly do hate to lose it. Can you go into a trance or look into a glass ball and tell me where that darned thing has got to?"

"If I could do anything like that do you suppose I would be living on a college professor's salary?"

These frank people who ask you impossible questions are not as bad as the quiet hero-worshippers. They silently and solemnly listen to the most trivial utterances of the psychologist as though the oracle were speaking again.

Perhaps just one thing more can increase the psychologist's embarrassment and that is to insist that he explain spiritualism. To a psychologist who has spent years in laboratories working on definite and detailed problems, the assumption that his interests have to do with ghosts and goblins puts his teeth on edge. As a matter of fact the psychologist along with the physiologist and biologist belongs in a laboratory.   He spends his life with instruments of precision.   They are his daily companions.   He works with them, they work upon him.   Gradually he acquires the feeling that he must have accuracy and precision.   No greater crime can he commit than that of incorrect observations and inaccurate comparisons. Naturally, the sort of thing that usually goes under the head of psychic research gives him an attack of indignation.

In view of the fact that what is presented in these pages percolates through the mind of a psychologist, it might be worth while to take a brief glance at the psychology of to-day.   Such a hasty impression can be best made by a brief excursion into a laboratory.

Professor Münsterberg of Harvard used to say that every psychological laboratory had to have at least two instruments, a chronoscope and a kymograph, just as every kitchen must have a stove and a frying pan.   For years the chronoscope has been used in all sorts of experiments.   It is an electric clock which runs only while a current is running through it, and it measures time in thousandths of a second.

Time is the essence of a large number of experiments.   One of the first of these was made to determine how long it takes to see a flash of light and make a response. This is known as "reaction time" and we find that it requires about two hundred and twenty thousandths of a second to make such a re-action. During the War the French and the Italians used to run their young men through such tests to determine whether they were sufficiently alert to become aviators. In the air service there are just two sorts of men, the quick and the dead. Our scientists thought that the reaction time was not a very good cue. Any one can be quick in doing the wrong thing. We ran our men through a discrimi-nation test in which they had to recognize a certain signal and make a certain reaction. This usually took them about five hundred thousandths of a second and strangely enough they could be quick and accurate even when they had been subjected to an inadequate supply of air and were suffering from oxygen starvation. Now this is the kind of problem the psychologist enjoys. He can vary his conditions quite accurately and can time the responses of the man upon whom he is experimenting very nicely.

Another use of the chronoscope is to detect how quickly one can speak a word in response to a single word given by the experimenter. This apparatus you may see in all psychological laboratories. A diaphragm is placed before the face of the experi-menter, and another before the person who is being tested. Wires connect both of the diaphragms with the chronoscope. The instant the stimulus word is spoken by the experimenter an electric connection is made and the chronoscope starts running. When the response is spoken the connection is broken and the clock stops. Alert college students will take about six hundred thousandths of a second in making a response. Such an accurate measurement of time will show up the least hesitancy in giving a word associated with the one the experimenter calls out. Any deliberation, confusion, or embarrassment results in a time longer than the student's average.

The kymograph is a slowly rotating cylinder upon which is placed some paper covered with lampblack. The slightest touch makes a white mark upon the soot. Resting against this smoked surface are several very light markers. As they move they write upon the black surface. Simple devices are made to show the heart-rate and the breathing-rate by lines on the smoked drum. As a person reads, listens to music, or gives his attention to a conversation, you can notice the difference in the lines being traced on the drum. One very interesting experiment illustrates how our throats, palates, and tongues are constantly making little movements as we think. A bulb can be placed well back in the mouth with a light rubber tube running from it to a marker alongside the kymograph. With each slight movement in the mouth this marker will register on the drum. Let a student be sitting and quietly reading, utterly unconscious of any activity of his speech organs the kymograph proves that he is indulging in a sort of incipient speech.

As I think of our laboratory some other instruments seem to present themselves for recommendation. A tone variator makes an impressive appearance. It supplies a very pure note. Should you tarry in the laboratory an obliging psychologist might have you listen to its dulcet tone and tell you that it was middle C on the piano. Then he might say that if you would close your eyes, listen carefully and tell him when the note has changed he would inform you how good an ear you have for discriminating pitch. If you noticed a change in pitch when the instrument was producing two hundred and fifty-eight vibrations he might congratulate you. If it read two hundred and seventy before you noted any difference he might suggest that the only instruments you should attempt to play are the bagpipe or the bass drum.

If the little experiment with the musical note aroused your curiosity you might be interested to know how good your hearing was for very high tones. Then your cicerone would probably take you to a little rack upon which hang numerous steel bars. Each is of a length to give an exact number of vibrations per second. Perhaps at eighteen thousand or at twenty-one thousand you may not be able to hear the little ringing tone when a cylinder is struck. There, then, is your limit for hearing high notes.

So we could saunter through the laboratory finding one device after another for making neat and accurate records of human traits and abilities. As far as possible every person who is studied is observed by means of machinery. You can trust a machine for accuracy. However, the machine cannot do all of the work. Many observations are impossible to measure by machinery.

Just here I cannot refrain from calling your attention to two kinds of psychology. One is based on laboratory methods; the other is based upon general observation and is largely the result of the individual's opportunities, interests and beliefs. When a psychologist makes a statement concerning musical ability you can have a great deal of confidence in what he says. When he makes a statement about the younger generation's abilities to make successful homes, take it with a liberal allowance of salt.

Good observation is indispensable for good psychology. We must stop and study this matter a little more carefully. Observation is fundamental to all science. As methods of observation improve, science expands. With the telescope and microscope and with improved photography, science has expanded her borders enormously. Moreover, habits of careful observation have made the science of today much more accurate than ever before.

You see there are three steps in the making of any science. The first is Observation which supplies the facts. Then Classification which analyzes and assorts the facts. And finally Explanation which deduces some principle or law governing the facts because of the way they classify.

An illustration will make this clear. You have probably noticed that when you glance from one eye to the other as you observe your eyes in the mirror you cannot see them move. When you read, your eyes move with a series of short jumps. You can easily notice this in anyone reading from a wide page. If you will put your finger beneath the line you are reading and move it slowly to the right across the page, you will notice that all the letters blur, as your eyes follow your finger-tip. Certainly the page does not blur as your eyes make those quick movements in reading. After these two simple observations, you are ready to go on with a little experiment. Spin a friend around on a piano stool a dozen times and then watch his eyes as he looks across the room. Notice how they jump quickly in one direction and not quite so quickly in another. How does the room look to him? It seems to go swimming by in one direction. But his eyes move in first in one direction and then the other, so you would expect the room to move first one way then quickly in the opposite way. From these observations we make our own classification of eye movements and decide that the eyes do not see anything when they move very quickly. We might jump to the conclusion that the eye becomes

blind when it makes a very quick movement, for
certainly we do not see. Now it becomes necessary
to make some observations. These must be done
with a great deal of care. We place our friend with
his head in a firm rest and before him we place a
screen which moves as rapidly as he spins. We
notice that he does see the screen when it moves as
quickly as his eyes do. So we must throw away our
former conclusion that he is blind during quick eye
movements. Can we find any other facts to put in
our classification of eye movements? Yes, we can
find people whose eyes do not move together. One
eye may be fixed on an object and the other may wander. This should present them with two sets of
objects, but it does not. They see only the object
upon which the one eye is steadily fixed and the
blurred image from the other eye is completely ig-
nored. From this we conclude that the mind cannot
use blurred images and completely inhibits them.
This would be a principle or a law in the psychology
of vision, but we never should have found it if we
had not been able to make a large number of observations and some of them under very carefully controlled conditions.

Subtly the sort of training a man has builds up
habits of thinking. Such habits direct the workings
of his mind. Though he feels ever so free in working
out his problems, he always keeps within the track of
his tried and proved procedures. Above all else he

is convinced that whatever field he is studying in
nature or human nature he has to deal with real
facts. This is the outcome of years of contact with
nature. Her facts may deceive him but he always
finds that the deception was a mistake that he had
made. Moreover, he acquires the habit of thinking
honestly. Attacks that he makes upon nature's
mysteries are frontal attacks, open and obvious.
Never does he assume that his success will depend
upon his ingenuity in some sort of a surprise attack,
some clever flank movement. Whatever may be the
complexities in any problem that science presents,
no scientist has ever drifted into the habit of thinking
that nature has a concealed ingenuity for tricking
him. True, some biologists have urged that there is
some sort of an intelligent direction in evolution,
but no one ever has endowed it with the mischievous
intent of playing jokes on scientists. Naturally
therefore the scientist has a very hard time when he
encounters the "facts" presented by magicians or
spiritualists. Let me illustrate.

A friend of mine took me into his back parlor, set
me on a divan, and told me that he was going to
show me how mind could control matter. This was
to be done by making four cards arise out of a pack
standing in a tall glass tumbler. A pack of cards
was fanned out before me, faces down, and I selected
four. My friend turned to the table to put the cards

in the tumbler. As he did so he exclaimed, "Oh, have you seen this?" and handed me a fan made of peacock feathers which had been lying on the table. When I picked it up, it seemed to fall into shreds. Then my friend took it and shook it and again it was a peacock fan. Laughingly he tossed it on the divan and said, "Let's go on with our experiment." He put the pack in the tumbler. Standing back from the tumbler on the little table, he told me to think of the first card I had drawn. As I did so that card rose up out of the pack and fell on the table. So each card popped up and flopped down on the table as I sat staring at that tumbler and thinking of them.

All through this performance my eyes and my attention were on the obvious things my friend was doing. They should have noted that the four cards selected were "forced." That is, they were, before me, slightly longer than any of the others and they also were marked on their edges. Then I should not have looked straight at that fan but should have kept my eyes on that pack. For it went into his left hand pocket and another came out of his right hand pocket with a thread looped under each of the cards that were about to perform. While I was staring at the fan wrecking itself, that pack was being placed in the tumbler and the little black thread was being tossed on the floor. Then while the cards were making their appearance one by one I should have been watching the movements of my friend's foot on the floor, for as each card rose his foot moved back about three inches.

Before I dared observe a good medium doing his work, I took a number of lessons in magic, all of which ran counter to my laboratory training. When I attempted a séance myself, I could readily see the necessity of doing the important thing while my friends were observing the unimportant. Thus I needed my hat near me in order to use it as a shield for reading face cards in the dark. How to get at that? Simple. I am a little late to the séance. All the chairs are taken except my own. I bustle in a little embarrassed at keeping them waiting, pull my chair out, push the table in position, give it a few turns, push it into another position, measure the distance from it to my chair with my eye—all of which seems very significant. Then toss my hat and coat to one side and again fix the chair and the table and apologize for being late. I am ready to go. When I want that hat, I have the group sing the "Battle Hymn of the Republic," so they will not hear my chair squeak as I reach for the hat. You can be sure that no one will notice that the hat is not lying in the same position, when the lights go on, as it was when I took my seat and started the séance.

Houdini once told me that he could do any trick that he could see performed three times. On the first occasion he merely noted what it was all about, in a general way; the second appearance found him ready to observe details that were important to the result but were unnoticed before, and the third time gave more of the obscure data and enabled him to test out theories that the second show had suggested.

I had been asking him how the famous Margery had obtained some of her effects and he pointed out that a good performer does not use the same method continously to obtain the same effects. Just when you feel sure that you have discovered the plan, it changes and you believe you were on the wrong track all along. That is art!

Never shall I forget the scorn he used in replying to my remark that I had seen Margery levitate a basket with hands, feet and head fastened.

"You *saw*, you say. Why you didn't see anything. What do you see now?"

With that, he took a half dollar, slapped it between the palms of his hands. It completely disappeared. As he was stripped to the waist, sleeves, pockets, and coat-linings were all ruled out. I had no idea how that coin had been so completely deflated so I asked for two repetitions. Of course, he refused.

Of course the ideal thing would be to train men in scientific work, in the study of magic and also in observing and reporting the so-called psychic phenomena. This, indeed, is just exactly what some of the societies for psychical research have done. However, a man employed by such societies, no matter how honest and conscientious he may be, is under a sort of restraint. In my observation such societies are not supported, to any extent, by scientific people. Rather, the money comes from people who are anxious to prove the existence of immortality by means of spiritualism. Any secretary who can find in the affirmative with a show of scientific precision is decidedly *persona grata*. If, on the other hand, he cannot find anything that even savours of mystery, he gradually discovers that he is thought of as inefficient.

Practically, therefore, we have to turn to men who are under no compulsion, overt or covert. This does not mean that we can pick any man of scientific training, teach him magic and turn him loose in a séance. He, too, may be under a compulsion. Well may he fear the reception of his report by his fellow scientists if he does not find a scientific explanation for everything he encounters. Nevertheless, there are a number of men who are known by their colleagues and who would give an honest report no matter what it might contain. Indeed I know some of them who would take a keen delight in finding something that would mystify their associates. So many exposures of trickery have been made that no one gets any pleasure out of adding to the list. If a few well-established, supernormal phenomena could be accurately observed, there are many able scientists who would keenly relish reporting them.

Among men of scientific training it does seem that the psychologist is rather better fitted for psychic research than the others.   In the first place he has to be trained in several sciences before he is at home in his own.   Biology is a broad introduction to psychology.   Its point of view and methods of research are familiar to the psychologist.   Physics and mechanics are indispensable in laboratory psychology. Nowadays a training in mathematics is necessary before attempting the statistical methods which are used in so much psychological work.

In addition to this nearly every active psychologist becomes very versatile.   If you will turn to a copy of the *Psychological Index* you will find psychologists engaged in every imaginable undertaking.   They train rats, remove parts of their brains and discover some curious things.   They measure the number of words a child of six carries in his repertory.   They photograph the movements of a rooster's eyes when he is dizzy.   They estimate the intelligence of everything from the genius to the congressman.   They select employees for different departments in the great stores.   They devise ingenious methods of teaching children.   Through it all runs the same adherence to careful observation, accurate comparison and cautious conclusions.

Inasmuch as the psychologist is the only scientist who is directly interested in what is called "consciousness," it would seem that he is just the man to tell us whether there is anything resembling intelligence in the curious phenomena that goes under the heading of Psychic Research. He should be able to tell whether there is any sense in the antics of a tilting table, the performance of the planchette board or the flickers of psychic lights. Certainly there is no other scientist whose subject trains him so well for the study of whether an independent intelligence controls the pencil of an automatic writer, or a separate intelligence speaks through the lips of a medium.

CHAPTER II

SCIENCE AND SEANCES

IN THE fall of 1925 I was enjoying a leave of absence
from Princeton University when an invitation
came to meet a committee from the American Society
for Psychical Research. It seems that a number of
the men in the Society felt that a psychologist with
laboratory training would be the type of man to
carry on the sort of investigations in which they were
interested. With some reluctance I met the committee, expecting to find gentlemen with long hair and
wild eyes. No one of the sort greeted me. Two
very able lawyers, a successful business man and an
astute young physician made it clear to me that they
wanted psychic phenomena treated by a scientist
using as rigid methods as science can use. I remarked to these gentlemen that the outcome would
probably show that no spiritistic hypothesis was
necessary to explain the things they had been studying. They laughingly remarked that they did not
care what my ideas were concerning hypotheses. All
that they wanted was an honest study of the facts.
After I had encountered some of the things they had
observed, they thought it was possible that I might
conclude that some of them were brought about by

forces which science had not yet classified or explained. Such an attitude would appeal to any fair-minded man. No strings were tied to me in any way. I was given perfect freedom and more generous pay than any university dreamed of at that time.

Knowing that accurate observations were indispensable, my first concern was to find some way of observing what goes on in a room that is absolutely dark. As you know, all spiritualists claim that rays of light destroy spirit phenomena. Only when there is a very strong psychic force can a little red light be permitted. Photography seemed to be the best solution Ether waves longer than those which give us red light and shorter than those which give us violet cannot be seen with the human eye. Of course they are totally invisible in a dark room. The infra-red rays take a little longer than the ultra-violet to register on a film. So I bought a camera with a film pack and equipped it with a quartz lens. Then I obtained a good mercury arc lamp and placed a filter over it so that I could fill a room quite nicely with ultra-violet light which could not be seen. After some experiments, I was able to take a picture of a medium in the dark quite nicely.

Once I was photographing a medium who claimed that he occasionally had ectoplasm exude from his body. He was skeptical about its appearing in an ultra-violet light, but he was perfectly willing to be photographed. I focused my camera in the lighted room upon his chair and then placed him in position, turned out the light, and made exposures from time to time. When I developed these, I was surprised to see a line of what appeared to be arrow heads which came from the side of the picture and vanished at a point in his chest. There were two lines that converged upon his chest. As I had done quite a little photographing and had never seen anything of the sort, I could not explain it. At one of the largest photography-supply houses they told me that the arrow heads were not due to defect in photography; that is, I had made no mistakes in exposing or developing my films. Inasmuch as I had bought the films, kept them carefully, and developed them myself I knew there was no trickery in the matter. Then I found a gentleman who had invented some photographical devices and knew the subject thoroughly. He too declared that the arrow heads were not due to faulty photography but were actually images of something which had been in existence in the room. That was disconcerting. Another specialist in photography who had been photographing operations for surgeons and who knew the tricks of cameras very intimately, also agreed that I had taken a picture of some *objects*. His remarks were amusing—"Doctor, I wish I could tell you what those things are. My mother-in-law is a spiritualist and nearly drives me crazy. Anything I could do to show it up I would do gladly, but hang it all, you have a picture of something there."

Several members of the Society suggested that I write an article and publish it in the magazine. They seemed to feel that this was probably the way in which a medium stocked himself up with psychic energy. One naïvely compared it to a water spout supplying the clouds with moisture. I was desperate.

My own prints were not artistic so I took my films to the Eastman place and had some excellent prints made. When the girl handed them to me over the counter, I remarked, "Look here. Now you have never seen anything as strange as this, have you? See these little pollywogs swimming out of space, and diving into the gentleman's wishbone?"

"Well, it is a little peculiar," remarked the young lady. "In all the years I have been here I have only seen two other cases of this. The last one made a gentleman very mad. He had these funny little things flying all over the board-walk at Atlantic City. We sent it to the laboratory and they made a study of it. I can get you their reports."

That report was surprising. When a picture is taken, using a film pack, a little current of electricity can be generated when the paper is torn from the pack. It does no harm unless there is a defect in the film. Even then it may run along the defect and not affect the picture unless the film has been under-exposed and over-developed. Such a thing may happen once in several thousand times. Imagine it! Of all the pictures I have ever taken this com-

bination of chances had to occur just when I was taking a medium in a dark room.

I am dwelling on this at some length because much
is made of photography in spiritualists' circles.
Amateurs can get some weird results. A man sitting with his back to a brick chimney may appear
in his photograph to have a halo around his head.
This has nothing to do with his saintliness. It is a
puzzle in physics. An amateur spiritualist found the
shadow of a mystic key lying across a picture of a
meadow. This gave him material for profound
thought. Prosaic explanation: a key had been left
lying on the paper of films in a strong light and had
made its impression before the film entered the camera.

Spirit photographs of little fairies playing tag under
toadstools and motherly faces looking in through the
window have their explanations not with the tricks
the camera plays on the photographer but just the
other way around.

Though my efforts did not yield anything but a
novel experience, it is certainly true that photography
is going to be the way of making records of what happens in the séance. Since my experiment photography with the ultra violet ray has made enormous
progress. Emulsions have been perfected so that we
now have films that are astonishingly sensitive. It
would not be at all difficult to fit up a room for a
séance flooded with ultra violet rays, which would

leave the room entirely dark and place a moving picture camera so that it would command a view of the whole room. Under these conditions we could be reasonably confident that most of the movements of the medium and his confederates can be recorded. Possibly small and quick movements would not register but we should certainly get some account of the medium moving in his chair, extending his reaching rod, waving his trumpet or crawling across the floor.

If you attempt to try such an experiment prepare yourself to exercise some patience. You will find little problems· popping up here and there that will tax your ingenuity. It will not be easy to locate your camera so that it may picture the movements of a confederate's foot. Intervening bodies will have a way of masking just what you want to record. Moreover, the ultra violet rays do some very funny things. They will impinge upon many objects and not reflect at all. Upon others they will strike and give you a surprising result. For example they will make the whites of the eye and the enamel of the teeth quite visible. I shall never forget my first experiments in a dark room with a friend. Alice in Wonderland never saw anything so grotesque. A pair of white eyes and a broad smile came through the dark toward me. Something was the matter with the smile. Where a front tooth should be there was a dark space. It seems that the ultra violet ray distinguishes between real teeth and their artificial mates. I also found that various and sundry objects would become visible. But it would not be difficult to rule these out or to cover them with a dark cloth.

What is said in a séance is really more significant than what is done. Swinging trumpets and flickering lights, baby fingers tweaking your ear and strange hands tugging at your trousers do not intrigue intelligent people very much. On the other hand a message purporting to come from someone dead but well known to a sitter may have very great significance. Many times I have known intelligent and educated men to ignore the so-called physical phenomena but to weigh the strange message they received with a good deal of interest.

Many things happen in the giving and receiving of messages that quite escape the attention. Compare the recollection of a half a dozen people of what actually occurred in a séance. You will be surprised to discover how different their memories are. This is in part due to faulty memory, but it is more largely due to faulty observation. One statement was more impressive to some one sitter than anything else. This he remembers and insists upon, though others have but a dim memory of it. Surely, there is nothing peculiar to the séance in all this. We find the same sort of thing whenever a number of people are called upon to give testimony.

Much more subtle than the tricks of memory and

impressions are the tricks one's own mind will play. Time and again I have listened to a quite intelligent sitter whose voice gave the medium many cues. As he became interested in what he was saying he forgot all about how he was saying it. Rising inflections would creep in to show the medium that the scent was hot. Little pauses in making a reply, quick responses which showed interest, all played into the hand of the medium and the sitter never realized what he was doing.

To make an analysis of how a message is delivered it is necessary to have all of the data. That is, there should be a record of each word spoken by the medium and the sitter, and also the inflections of the voice, the pauses, the interruptions, the quick responses. With this in mind I tried to construct an apparatus which would record everything said in the séance. It was to be a combination of a dictaphone and dictagraph with a device for registering time. It would not work. It was necessary to have one speak directly into the mouthpiece to get a good record. Now you simply cannot go racing around a dark room, filled with people, trying to bring the mouthpiece to the end of a trumpet that plays tag all over the place. To-day, however, with the development of the microphone it would be possible to get a pretty good record of what happens in those exchanges between medium and sitter.

Few experiments can be made with instruments only. Somewhere in making observations, classifying them and drawing conclusions the human element must enter. Throughout science the influence of this human element is known as the "personal equation." Years ago when astronomers were observing movements of the heavenly bodies they found that some astronomers made their records read slightly later in observing their phenomena than did others. This led to a study of the length of time it took to see a flash of light and to record a reaction. So it was one of the first studies in reaction time. It showed that there were differences between individuals. The personal equations of some caused their records to indicate that certain performances in the heavenly bodies were not being conducted on time.

In the mathematical or physical sciences there is less opportunity for the personal equation to creep in than in such subjects as psychology and economics. However, I have known a maker of scientific instruments who maintained that one of his worst troubles was the personal equation in so simple a thing as measuring the length of a steel bar. Many times the bar must be measured and then an average taken to get a fine accuracy. Now when a man finds his average is slightly larger than a number of others made by other men he begins to get shorter readings in his own measures. No dishonesty is involved.

His efforts are as serious and careful as before but they show, some times to his surprise, that he is getting different results.

Mental tests, among the psychologists, often show the effect of the personal equation. I recall one experimenter who prided himself on the accuracy of his work and his ability to detect subnormal children. When his results were compared with others it became evident that his technique was too severe. On the other hand a psychologist who was particularly partial to little girls found so few of them subnormal that his colleagues became suspicious and claimed he could not resist his personal equation.

In fact the more play the individual's judgment has the more liable he is to inject his personality into his study. For this reason the reports of many social workers are undependable. For example, a problem which has worried us for a long time is the inheritance of mental troubles. If we rely entirely upon the hospital records for patients whom they have treated we could not possibly make up a family tree. For this reason trained social workers try to visit as many members of the patient's family as possible. They go out into the highways and byways and trace out as many family connections as they can. Suppose the worker is convinced that all mental disorders are inherited. Then we are apt to find any peculiar aunt or uncle or any crochety great-grand-parent listed among those members of the family that gave evidence of mental defect. Should the worker, on the

other hand, be convinced that only the most flagrant
cases of insanity have hereditary connections, then
we would probably find the same peculiar and crotch-
ety people listed among the normals.

However, we need not despair of getting some
pretty good material from trained observers; material
that we can really depend upon. Moreover, we can
gauge the certainty of our material. It is accom-
plished in this way. Each observer makes a careful
record. These records are compared by means of a
mathematical formula and we can tell exactly how
well they agree. During the war we devised a
number of experiments to test the abilities of aviators.
After we had graded the cadets it was a question
whether our tests were any good at all. To prove
their value we had several flying officers rate the
cadets as to their actual ability in managing planes.
Facts we could not get at were well known to these
officers,—whether their men made bad landings, flew
with one wing down, climbed too steeply, misjudged
distances, showed bad judgment; or whether they
remembered their instructions at all times and performed accordingly. Fortunately these officers agreed
and we found a good correlation between their records. If the cadets had to be scored on their performances by men who could not decide in their own
minds what constituted a good take-off, good control
of the plane, and a good landing, we should never
have found a correlation in their observations.

Speaking of army officers making accurate observations of a soldier's abilities, I cannot refrain from calling your attention to the Officer's Rating Scale. Periodically an officer had to rate other officers whom he knew for their ability. Such traits as leadership, general intelligence, personal qualities and value to the service were given numerical values, similar to a student's marks in college. When a large number of these had been collected it was possible to form a fair idea of a man. Sometimes an individual report would obviously flatter the man too much or condemn him badly. I recall one report that an officer made upon one of his fellows after a bitter argument in which he had been clearly worsted. In his report he credited his former opponent with fifty-three per cent of the intelligence that an officer should have. I have no doubt that this officer was conscientious and did not imagine that his personal equation crept into the record at all.

In addition to using the correlation formula for testing the accuracy of a number of observers, the scientist often finds that another mathematical device helps him to evaluate observations. That is the distribution curve. By it he can estimate what an average is for a number of observations and what deviations occur. This gives an idea of the accuracy of the work. Moreover, in a number of cases he can work out according to the rules of probability just how improbable some remarkable phenomena may be.

No place in all the realm of human experience does

the personal equation show more clearly than in the observations made in a séance. Never shall I forget a civil engineer who had excellent scientific training report how he saw a trumpet rise from the floor with nothing touching it. So thoroughly was he convinced that spiritual forces could move crass matter that all his scientific training deserted him in the presence of this illusion. Every medium is keenly alive to the personal equations of his sitters. The best séances I have ever seen were held when a number of uncritical and sympathetic people were present. I recall one made up entirely of women, most of them "believers," and all of them with someone whom they had loved that had died. Helpful messages from those whom they identified were plentiful, gentle spirits tossed flowers to them and spirit hands gave them friendly touches. The same medium had little or nothing to give when a group of critical men were present. Naturally every report of what happens in a séance is coloured by the personal equation. I cannot remember any occasion where three or four careful observers kept accurate notes of what they saw and heard and then sought a correlation for their records. Obviously that is just the sort of thing that is necessary. Nothing distorts our observation so badly as the play of our emotions. Be a little apprehensive, a little nervous and see what a disconcerting story you will tell your friends. I have known a man who thought everything connected with spiritualism a thorough-going fake; yet, when he heard what purported to be a message from his father, he could not make a good detailed report of what the medium said or what he had replied.

There are not many situations so difficult for good observation as the séance. To begin with the darkness is disturbing to many people. They are not accustomed to it for it is much darker than their unlighted rooms at night. Some of them carry over a little of the haunting fears of the dark of their childhood. Added to this their composure is not improved by having a clammy finger touch their faces. In fact the whole setting makes against a good observation. Things happen most unexpectedly when everyone is singing or talking. Their minds are diverted. Uncertainty and expectancy become contagious. An exclamation of surprise or fright easily disturbs a person who might otherwise have kept his composure. Often one waits for ten or fifteen minutes and nothing happens. Then when he has become discouraged and relaxes his vigilance a psychic light may flash in one side of the room, or a trumpet touch him on the forehead, so unexpectedly that he can hardly describe the occurrence at all. Constrained positions with hands joined and feet flat on the floor become irksome. Indeed there is nothing in the séance to help the naïve. If he has no training to cope with the situation, what he sees, hears and describes are just about worthless.

CHAPTER III

A GREAT MEDIUM

MEDIUMS specialize. Some insist upon one sitter at a time, some insist upon a group. The technique differs for the two types.

Among the greatest of group mediums that I met was Cartheuser. On this I have been reassured by some of the oldest members of the American Society for Psychical Research. "In thirty years I have not encountered so excellent a medium," said one of the wealthiest and most widely experienced members who had had an opportunity of studying mediums here and abroad. When I first met Cartheuser, I was impressed by his appearance,—rather under-sized, quite retiring, with pale blue eyes, and a harelip. He was also said to have a cleft palate. In speaking, his labials were blurred and his gutturals as well. Nothing could be more dreadful than trying to get a message from him over the telephone. His voice was about the usual range for male voices and had no distinctive overtones that would distinguish it from other male voices. In conversation he was always diffident and reticent, giving the impression that he was nervous and apprehensive.

In private conversations I gathered from this re-

markable medium that he was of Pennsylvania Dutch
extraction and that he had worked as an automobile
mechanic. Acting as a medium was something he
had taken up when he discovered he "possessed
psychic power." He had a wife and two of the most
attractive children I have ever seen. Conversing
about things in general he showed very good judgment and in discussing mechanics he displayed some
ingenuity. However, his professional appearance
gave no indication of an alert mind. On the contrary
he seemed rather dull and stupid. A number of people remarked that he had not the mental ability to
think quickly and improvise "messages."

If you will read the literature, you will find that
many reports describe the medium as being dull or
feeble-minded, implying that any remarkable or brilliant effects in their works could not be due to their
own ingenuity. Naturally, it is a great help to a
medium to have his followers believe that anything
strikingly clever cannot be due to *his* efforts.

I must confess that I acquired quite a fondness
and admiration for this able little medium. Time
and again I have seen his talent pitted against the
hostile criticism of hard-headed business and professional men. I must confess that I did derive some
pleasure in hearing some of these hostile critics ac-
knowledge their bewilderment after a séance with
Cartheuser. In particular, one very ingenious young

engineer who was splendidly trained in science dropped into a séance one evening for the purpose of explaining how the tricks were done and gloating over a friend who was badly perplexed by the whole thing. After the performance he took me aside and said, "Doctor, what is the low-down on this thing? I don't just get it. Of course I know it's fake but I don't see how." Nor was he alone. Keen lawyers, doctors, and business men often expressed themselves in much the same way.

A typical séance with Cartheuser, as staged for us, was about as follows. The room used was my own study and I knew there were no tricks or gadgets concealed on the premises. It was made completely dark so that you could pass your hand immediately in front of your eyes and see no change in the darkness. From the ceiling hung an electric lamp on a long cable in such a way that it cleared the floor by a few inches. Around the light a shield kept all the rays from distributing through the room and several layers of paper dimmed the light down so that there was only a faint illumination on the floor. In this illuminated area sat a bowl with water. Often flowers were placed in it by the ladies. On either side he usually placed a trumpet. One was surrounded with a band of luminous paint, which could be seen in the dark for sometime after the séance started. Around the bowl some ten or twelve chairs would be placed in a circle. After all precautions had been taken to prevent any light seeping through the cracks, the séance was ready to proceed.

An average performance would start with some instruction to the sitters concerning their behavior. They were assured that the medium could not guarantee any results at all as he could not control the powers which governed him. Each sitter could contribute something to the success of the sitting by conforming to rules that had proven practical. One of these was to sit in his chair with both feet flat on the floor. Another was to unite hands around the circle when requested by the medium. A third was to join in singing when requested. A fourth was to avoid being tense, to relax and be natural.

No solemn nor lugubrious air pervaded a Cartheuser meeting. On the contrary the attitude of the people and the character of the conversation were quite cheerful, sometimes running into hilarity. This is quite to the credit of the medium. When one walks through a graveyard he acquires an attitude that does not make for giving or receiving very sensible ideas. Moreover, the messages that Cartheuser brought were not of the kind to bring tears into the eyes of a stone image. He refrained from the pathetic scenes of a mother's last few minutes and those harrowing details of the little child's last sickness. Jokes were not uncommon. Not a few of the cheerful spirits that whispered through his trumpets would essay a *jeu d'esprit*. Such an atmosphere appealed to sensible men and women.

To a newcomer in such a séance the first surprise came by way of the trumpets. The luminous trumpet could be seen by means of the band painted with luminous paint. The dark trumpet was invisible throughout the séance. At the beginning the luminous trumpet would rise leisurely from the floor, the mouth of it swinging in the direction of Cartheuser's seat. Apparently the "spirit" lifting it pointed the mouth towards the medium. Then this trumpet seemed to float around the room. It could be seen high in the air. Indeed, it seemed to touch the ceiling which was about eight feet from the floor. Then it would swing around, seemingly darting from one corner of the room to another. Sometimes it would sweep around the circle with a loud, swishing noise, barely missing the noses of the sitters. One could not help wondering why some nose was not injured. Such wonder increased as the trumpet settled down and began approaching different members of the group. With the greatest nicety it would float up alongside of one's ear and a faint voice could be heard whispering through it. Quite remarkable were some of its antics. Time and again the mouth of it would stop so short a distance from my face that a little push forward would bring my forehead in contact with it. Once in a while it would give me a friendly little bump on the top of my head by way of repartee.

But its greatest accuracy was displayed in gently touching one sitter's eyeglasses.

As you sit in the dark and think about these performances it may occur to you to reach out and touch your neighbor's ear or nose, by way of testing how accurately your hand can move in the dark. I tried this. Most disconcerting were the results. If I aimed at an ear I was quite apt to touch a chin or the back of a head. Even a swinging movement of the palm of the hand aimed at a nose may net you a chin or a forehead. It is well to have a good natured neighbor. It is well also, to have a good deal of self composure, for you are going to discover in such an experiment that you have no accuracy at all. Then you ask yourself just what is steering that trumpet. Surely the medium cannot see in the dark; no one can. Even in daylight these movements would call for a good coördination between eye and hand.

Following the surprise from the trumpets there usually came no little surprise when voices spoke through them. Before the séance everyone had an opportunity to talk to Mr. Cartheuser and no one could fail to notice how badly he articulated. Those who had made any study of the voice and expression noted at once that the harelip gave the characteristic blurring of the labials. This was very apparent. Added to that the difficulty he had in pronouncing his gutturals made his speech so unusual that no one failed to remark it. However, when the voice of "Dr. Andrews" came through the trumpet no one could detect any defects in his articulation. He represented a family doctor of the old school. His voice was as deliberate and clear as anyone could wish. Quite amusingly it would conjure up a picture of the old-fashioned doctor with his inquiries about your ailments. Quite a different effect was produced when "Black Bear," the Indian, dropped in. "Dropped in" is quite the right expression. This voice came roaring down from the ceiling. Gruff and unconvincing was this ethereal aborigine. His broken English was pretty thoroughly fragmented but his labials and guturals were all right. Happily he did not come often. One meets altogether too many Indians at séances.

Far and away the most impressive voice that came through the trumpets was that of little "Elsie." It was splendid. Its articulation was clear and distinct and the range of the voice was that of a little girl of about twelve or fourteen years. It gave the impression of a girl's voice before it has "changed." When a boy's voice changes it may drop an octave or more. This occurs at the beginning of adolescence. Girls' voices also change but no so markedly. As one listened to Elsie's voice it seemed to retain its high childish soprano. It did not seem possible that Cartheuser could stretch his vocal cords to reach such high tones. Time and again different sitters would comment upon this unique feature. One singing teacher told me that the Elsie voice had overtones in it which were not like those of Cartheuser's voice. Of course the quaint little German accent that characterized it was not particularly convincing but it also gave a contrast to Cartheuser's language.

Those who heard Elsie speaking through the trumpet a number of times gradually built up in their imaginations a quaint little personality. Often she acted as the go-between for the sitter and some weak spirit who could not sound through the trumpet. Frequently she talked on her own behalf, always with a kindly, friendly manner. Now and then she would indulge in some bright repartee. Often she would show an interest and a sympathy for some sitter with whom she chose to talk. There seemed to be a very thorough consistency in the part she played. Always she maintained the same sort of childish, half-playful traits. I have talked with people some time after the séances and have found that they shared my impression of having heard a very distinct and attractive little personality present herself. In fact Elsie dwells in my mind with a good deal more clearness than a number of characters in fiction where the author had the clear intention of giving a good character portrayal. This, too, must be credited to the art of the medium. No stupid medium could produce a personality with the charm and the consistency of Elsie. Here then is a new form of art. It is neither literature, painting or sculpture. But it is a portrayal.

Occasionally, Elsie would give some startling messages. I recall one that seemed to me quite remarkable. Through the trumpet she held, with a very intelligent lady sitter, a conversation which ran about as follows:

Elsie: "An old gentleman is here. He says he wished to speak to you."

Sitter: "I shall be very glad to talk with him."

Elsie: "The old gentleman says that he is your father."

Sitter: "Splendid. I'd love to talk with him."

Elsie: "He says that you do not believe he is your father and that you would like some cue to prove it."

Sitter: "That would be fine."

Elsie: "The old gentleman says that the cue is 'shoes and leather.'"

Sitter: "That's a very excellent cue."

Elsie: "He says, why don't you go ahead and get that lace dress? Now he cannot stay longer. He is becoming weak— now he is gone."

After the sitting this lady explained the message. Her father was an elderly man and had trouble with his eye-sight sometime before he died. In chopping wood he missed his aim and hit his foot with the result that he had to have a special, small shoe made for the injured foot. Being a genial, humorous, old gentleman, he contended that it was all for the best— that he did not need so much leather for his shoes, an important economy. The lace dress was an interesting reference. This lady had been admiring a

lace dress but had felt that lace was unbecoming to
her. In her indecision she told the sales-girl to put
the dress aside. So neat and apt was this short
statement from Elsie that the lady could not help
feeling that there was something more than chance in
its remarkable contents.

On one occasion the trumpet drifted up beside my
ear and the following colloquy ensued:

Voice: "Hello, hello, hello."
Sitter: "Hello, who are you?"
Voice, faintly: "Har--."
Sitter: "Harry?"
Voice: "Harrow--."
Sitter, exclaiming: "Oh, Howard!"
Voice: "Yes, yes, yes."
Sitter: "Well old man this is great to have a word with you!"
Voice: "Sure, 'Howard.' How are the ladies? How are
stocks?"
Sitter: "I guess the ladies are all right but you know stocks."
Voice: "Ha! Ha! Ha! Like old times! So you got a letter
from Fred?"
Sitter: "Yes, at last! Do you know what was in the letter?"
Voice: "Sure! He told you all about his trip."
Sitter: "Where is Fred now?"
Voice: "He's in St. Louis. Well, good-bye, I can't hold on.
I've got to go."

This experience is recounted to the best of my ability. Since the experience occurred I have told that
incident a hundred times. I am not aware of adding
or subtracting anything. As honestly as I can state

anything, I repeat this experience. Nevertheless, I am confident that my own observation of what occurred and my memory of it do not accurately represent what occurred. In short I am confident that I am guilty of the usual faults, namely, remembering the striking and interesting things and forgetting items that might explain the success of the message; for this message was a success. The beginning of the message carries some suspicion. The voice was very faint and I guessed several names. Undoubtedly, I exclaimed "Howard" in a tone that indicated that name was significant. And indeed it was. One of my oldest friends whom I had known from boyhood had died a year or so prior to this séance. A mutual friend who had gone to school with both of us was "Fred." Neither of us had seen Fred for fifteen years and had never heard anything about him. He was an interesting and eccentric fellow who continually had unusual adventures. The statement that I had a letter from Fred was remarkable, for I had received a letter addressed by Fred to a mutual fried several months after Howard died. This letter contained a long account of Fred's experiences in the South Sea Islands. This impressed me very much at the time of the séance and stands out in my mind as the most remarkable thing in the incident. The statement that Fred was in St. Louis was simply a bold remark on the part of the medium for I had no way of checking up on that at the time. Several years later I learned that Fred had never been in St. Louis. The remarks about the ladies and the stocks seemed at the time peculiarly appropriate. This friend and I began going to see girls together as boys. We encouraged each other in our courtship. Later in life we considered ourselves connoisseurs of the fair sex. Nevertheless, such a remark could have come from a number of personal friends. The statement concerning stocks was also *a propos*. Many an argument we had concerning the merits of bonds and common stocks. That too, is a remark that many another friend might have made.

I have always valued the recollection of this experience for I find that it makes me quite sympathetic toward my fellow-men. When I hear remarkable accounts of a friend's experience with a medium, I can understand him better. Even after training myself in observations of both the medium and myself, I find that I have fallen into the same pitfall as others. I was surprised to hear the name of an old friend and my attention went to the content of the message and not to the inflections in my own voice or to hesitations in the spirit replies. If a man who sets himself the task of making accurate observations can slip up so badly, we must concede that all séances should be more accurately reported—if possible, mechanically reported.

One evening I invited a young doctor from Boston to attend a sitting. He had never been interested in any sort of psychic research and both his temperament and his training led him to regard it as childish and not even entertaining. Nevertheless he was somewhat intrigued by the fact that Dr. Crandon, a Boston physician, claimed that his wife was a medium. I had talked the Crandon case over with him and he showed enough interest to buy a stethoscope and urge me to put it on Mrs. Crandon's throat when her control was speaking. So I had him attend a Catheuser sitting while I was trying a stethoscope on that medium. I introduced him as Mr. Archer, nothing more. The following is a *stenographic* report of isolated statements by Elsie and occasional replies by Mr. Archer. Compare it with those recalled by memory.

> *Voice:* Hello.
> *Voice:* Louise.
> *Answer:* Yes.
> *Voice:* It is Louise.
> *Voice:* Not for you.
> *Voice:* Louise again. Mr. Archer asks if Louise is for him. Trumpet touches him.
> *Voice:* She's all right.
> *Voice:* Last name begins with "C".
> *Voice:* She loves you, loves you, loves you.
> *Voice:* I see mother, I often see her, she's not here.
> *Voice:* (Said something I didn't hear).
> *Mr. Archer:* She wants me to have children, etc.------
> *Voice:* No, no, no.
> *Voice:* Don't try to be foolish, try to be sensible and you will receive the truth.

Voice: She would never say that. Nobody would unless they were fresh.

Voice: Louise is still here.

Voice: Is Louise related to your mother?

Voice: She says she knows your mother.

Voice: She says something about two boys in your family. Mr. Archer answers that there are two boys in his family.

Voice: Do you know someone belonging to you by the name of Arthur?

Voice: Someone here calls that name and is related to you.

Voice: I'll try to tell her to talk a little clearer.

Voice: She also says something about someone in your family by the name of Bill.

Voice: There's someone here with the letters G. H.

Voice: There's someone here for you in a uniform.

Voice: Did you know someone by the name of G. Brown? He was a soldier wasn't he?—'cause he had a uniform on.

Voice: That's right—that's what he used to have, 351st Field Artillery.

Voice: I'll have to see what he says.

Mr. Archer: Is he happy?

Voice: Eddy—but that's not his name.

Voice: That's not your real name is it?

Voice: Know what he says? Something that you had to do with an old shack.

Voice: No—it looks like a barn.

Voice: Say Eddy, did you have something to do with pigeons?

Mr. Archer: I did have smething to do with chickens, etc.

Voice: I'll see if I can see any other boys you were in France with.

Voice: You have a trophy that belongs to someone, you swiped it. That's true, you must have taken it from a soldier.

Voice: It's something that looks like a medal.

Voice: If you know what it is say so.

Voice: That's all right. I appreciate it.

Voice: I know and there's something to it.

Voice: Have you anything that looks like a medal or trophy?

Answer: No.

Voice: Do you know anyone by the name of Foster?

Voice: He wasn't a soldier was he?

Voice: Do you know his first name?

Voice: I was going to say, Ed— E. Foster.   Just E. Foster there must be someone by that initial.

Voice: Did you know there were three women up there?

Voice: Say listen, Brownie sends his regards to you.

Voice: Do you wear a mustache?

Answer: No.

Voice: You have a sister too, but she's on earth.

Voice: There's someone here has something wrong with his foot, can hardly walk, walks with a stick.

Voice: That's what I thought—your grandfather.

Voice: Hello Professor.

Voice: Don't get too anxious.

Voice: Say Eddy, did you ever work in a restaurant or a hotel?

Voice: This party talks about it.

Answer: Yes.

Voice: Well isn't that funny.

Voice: Did you run around with towels.........

Voice: She talks about towels.

Voice: What do you call those dogs with............

Answer: Fox-terrier.

Voice: He's right in front of you here.

Voice: Do you see him Mr. Walton?

Voice: What did you call him?

Voice: Didn't I say Rick?

Voice: Chip is near enough.

Voice: Wait a minute I have to put something over the horn, you'll get all wet.

Voice: Here Rick!

Voice: Say Eddy, there's something the matter with his paw.
Voice: Say Eddy, he was not much of a barker.
Voice: (said something about Brownie).
Voice: Have you a watch chain that belongs to someone over there?
Voice: That's what I said.
Voice: Well why don't you try it.
Voice: Have you anyone by the name of Anna?
Voice: Someone sends their love to Anna.
Voice: Yes my boy, yes. (grandfather)
Voice: I guess it means your mother.
Voice: I'm all right now grandfather says.
Voice: Had trouble with his eye too.
Voice: Who's Charlie?
Voice: Grandpa wants to be remembered to Charlie.
Voice: Grandpa says something about a piece of leather.
Voice: Did he have something to do with leather?
Voice: He says Merry Christmas to all.
Voice: Says he was hurt by a horse, is that right?
Voice: He says something about jars of honey.
Mr. Archer: That's right about the honey.
Voice: God bless you.
Voice: Good-bye, grandpa.
Voice: Wasn't that nice?
Voice: That's what I call spiritual education.
Voice: It takes so long to hit the right.........
Voice: The least little thing upsets...........
Voice: Hello Eddy, what do you think of it?
Voice: I thought you didn't believe in spooks?
Voice: I say, did you hear Walter in Boston?
Voice: You never sat with him?
Voice: That's all.

In all this medley of statements there are some very nice hits mixed in with many misses. Indeed, the hits were so numerous that the doctor was quite puzzled. The fact that the medium mentioned the doctor in uniform, named a personal friend who had died during the war and had gotten the number of his regiment partly right was quite impressive. Added to that was the fact that he promptly spoke the name of someone very close to the doctor and followed it up by the name of his mother and sister. These items stood out so clearly that both the doctor and I rather forgot the irrelevant and insignificant things as we talked the séance over that night. Later, the reading of the stenographic notes gave me rather a shock when I saw how much material there was not really pertinent.

Many sittings gave far less interesting material than this. Indeed, a whole evening could be spent watching the trumpets and listening to such trifling things as these, which followed the interesting material given the doctor:

Voice: If I bring it through Monday, I'll try to bring it through Wednesday too.

Voice: What it is is a surprise.

Voice: We'll try, but we won't promise. I'll try my darndest.

Voice: Put out the old camera.

Voice: Just for that reason I want a camera.

Voice: I'll do it without a camera too.

Voice: Do you want to go home?

Voice: I'll let you know the time in about a minute and a half; in the meantime sing.

Voice: Somebody's watch is wrong.

Voice: Twenty minutes to eleven.
Voice to Mr. Archer: Your watch is about three minutes slow.
Answer: That's right.
Voice: You can turn on the red light.
Voice: If there's any more messages today, it's more money than anyone can pay for.
Voice: Listen here, Professor, when we were in Lily Dale we brought you something, so what are you kicking about.
Voice: You want the red light, you want messages, you want it all in five minutes.
Voice: Sings "What am I going to do."
Voice: Mrs. ——— doesn't want any messages to-night.
Voice: You'll be here to-morrow won't you.
Voice: Sing first, then turn the red light on.
Voice: Sing "Glory, Glory, Hallelujah."
Voice: Not ready for the red light yet
Voice: Says, yes, sing some more.   .
Voice: Now turn the light on.
Voice: Sings; trumpet whistled.
Voice: Sings, "Smile, smile, smile."
Luminous trumpet went right around the circle.
Voice: Did you use ear-horns? (to Dr. McComas)
Voice: Well, did you hear something.
Voice: May peace be with you.   I bid you all good-night.

The liveliest evening we had happened when all the sitters were ladies. The lamp suspended from the long cable began to swing. It threw its light upon the feet of the medium, at one side of the circle and then, upon the feet of the sitters—at the opposite side. Gradually, the swings became longer. Then the lamp swung over to Cartheuser and suddenly stopped, showing his hands resting upon his knees.

of herself very cleverly.   This was interesting because Miss X could not draw.   Then Annie told her story. She had been led astray by a man who had promised to protect her and she had died in misery, giving birth to a child.   She represented herself as having lived the life of a prostitute and had learned to hate men violently.   Annie's writing would be done with considerable vigor in a coarse, flowing hand with her arms stiff and the fingers tightly gripping the pencil. Occasionally she would bang her arm on the table and pound her feet on the floor.   During Annie's appearance Miss X's expression would seem to indicate some fright.   She would grit her teeth, press her lips firmly together, and raise her eyebrows.   This expression grew more marked toward the latter part of the experiment.

Mary Patterson was a personality more like that of Miss X than any of the others.   She appeared rather seldom and would be rudely thrust aside by the more aggressive ones   She used the best English and her handwriting was much like that of Miss X.

Mary Minott despised the gentle Mary Patterson, claiming that she was a prig and puritanical.   She would insist that if Miss X would only listen to her she would become a famous designer.   As a guaranty of this she drew some designs of a number of beautiful dresses—something of which Miss X was incapable in her normal condition.   Miss X's father who had died purported to be another personality and assumed the handwriting of her father. He did not often appear and when he did he confined himself to remarks about the family. Alton was a personality of a curious sort from the spiritualist's point of view, for he was a very much alive young man, the fiancé of one of Miss X's friends. She had met him the previous summer. He wrote in very sentimental terms and tried to dissuade her from marrying the man to whom she was engaged. He would urge her to give herself up to mediumship saying that both the dead and living spirits could speak through her. Surely it would be unique if we could have a sitting where a living Alton could read the automatic writing of his own spirit!

A sixth personality represented himself as the spirit of war and desolation. He sounded dreadful warnings and urged Miss X to go in for Red Cross work. It should be noted that this occurred just before America entered the world war.

The last personality to develop and the one who caused the disruption of the experiment presented himself as "Man." In the beginning he was not at all distinct, either in handwriting or in the matter of his messages. He would wander into irrelevant remarks and would give ambiguous answers. Eventually he identified himself as Man and would alternate with Alton. However, he acquired a dislike for Alton and finally drove him out of the experiment. He and Annie McGinnis did not get along at all together. These two personalities eventually held the field together, but Man became more persistent and dominating. He expressed a strong interest in dancing. This progressed to such an extent that Miss X said she could dance spontaneously if she gave herself up to the impulse. This she did on one occasion; getting to her feet she began to sway back and forth. The swaying became more violent, and she began to wave her arms and make a curious shuffling movement. Her body gave a violent wrench and she cried out in a sharp voice, her face depicting a struggle of emotions, ecstacy and terror. For ten minutes she lay stiff and moaning. When she returned to a normal condition she said that she had tried to control the movements and suddenly realized that she could not. She was in fear of losing herself and of another personality gaining control.

The second case is that of a Miss Z. She first began doing automatic writing during her freshman year in college as she knew her mother had written, and thought that she would try. Her automatic writing differed from that of Miss X, in that it never reproduced any recurring personality and also in that it continued after she married. Her work is in the nature of short stories. The first of these was written in one evening, purporting to come from one William Young, who declared that he had been born in England over a hundred years ago. His was a sad story. William was a butler to a wealthy family and he drew a magnificent picture of himself in his livery. All through, William illustrated the story with clever pictures. Miss Z, like Miss X had no ability in drawing. As the story unfolded, it appeared that the resplendent William and his brother were both in love with the same young lady. The story reaches its denouement and William's exit in a picnic. Here the wicked brother courteously passed some food to William, in which was an onion that had been poisoned. He strangled and died. The lady was terribly grieved but permitted herself to become first comforted and then wed by the wicked brother. They lived happy ever afterward to the great annoyance of William.

A more intriguing tale is that of Charles You, sent by the German government to China to make a geological survey in the interior. He was accompanied by an assistant, with whom he had a quarrel which ended in a fight. During the fight he received an injury in the foot and could not move for some time after regaining consciousness. Owing to the lack of proper medical attention an infection started which resulted in his death. One illustration appeared in this story which according to Dr. Mühl was most remarkable. Miss Z drew a picture of the bones of the human leg and foot. In the foot not a tarsal nor metatarsal was omitted and they were perfectly placed. This impressed Dr. Mühl as she was then studying anatomy and knew the great difficulty of drawing the bones in the foot. Miss Z had never

made such a study though she had seen the bones of
a skeleton in the laboratory. When she was asked to
make a conscious effort to draw what she had done
so perfectly in her automatic writing she was unable
to draw anything that resembled the skeleton of a
foot.

Miss Z neglected her automatic writing for some
time; then when Dr. Mühl visited her they attempted
an experiment. Miss Z sat at the table and made
some incoherent records with her right hand. Her
facility for smooth writing seemed to be lost. Dr.
Mühl took a pencil and put it into her left hand, saying, "Let's see what that will do." Almost immediately the left hand began writing coherent records.
A pencil was placed also in the right hand. There
seemed to be a momentary quiver in each arm and
both hands began writing at the same time, recording
a different message and each denoting a different
sex. In small characters the left hand wrote under
the name of Anita Glane. With bold flourishing
letters the right hand wrote for Daniel Raun. Soon
a conflict arose and the left hand retired from the con-
test writing "I want to be strong but I am weaker."
Then the right hand wrote all over the page in huge
letters the word "good."

As we review these remarkable records we are impressed by the fact that Miss X studied her own case
intelligently. She had been trained in psychology
and she tried to "introspect" in order to find out how

the curious personalities were built up. She readily
explained Annie McGinnis as a character that developed from her experiences in the social work. Annie was in part the expression of ideas of which Miss
X had once been acutely conscious. However she
could not at first explain the Alton personality. Only
after numerous attempts at self analysis did she recall a conversation with her mother. This seemed
to explain the character of his messages and when she
hit upon this explanation he gradually disappeared.
Dr. Mühl believes that the curious personality, Man,
which slowly developed represented a bi-sexual trend
in the subject and came if not wholly at least to a
great extent from the unconscious.

Miss Z presents a curious puzzle in writing with
both hands at the same time. We are not told anything about her introspection concerning the two
names that wrote simultaneously though we note that
the first name written by the left hand is that of Dr.
Mühl. I have also witnessed a case of automatic writing where the left hand wrote simultaneously with the
right but wrote the same material. How the centre
governing the movements of the left hand can write
differently from what the right hand is doing constitutes a nice problem.

Miss Z's ability to draw the bones of the foot so
accurately brings out a principle which is rather well
known. There are other cases where a subject has
given evidence that he retained very accurately what

he had perceived and could reproduce it in hypnosis. This makes clear to us that many of the remarkable descriptions in the automatic writings of reputed mediums are but the re-presentation of things they have retained but cannot recall ordinarily.

Dr. Mühl finds the explanation of the personalities and the clever stories in what is called the "para-consciousness." It is neither clear consciousness nor the unconscious. It would take us too far afield to explore such theories. We only note that there is a natural explanation and we do not have to resort to the supernatural.

I do not think we should close this chapter without warning the ambitious to be careful in their attempts at automatic writing. Nature has designed the whole nervous system to act in coöperation. One of the most important laws in the activities of consciousness is that it acts as a unity. Any practice that makes for a dissociation runs counter to nature and may result in some harmful effect.

CHAPTER V

WEIRD EXPERIENCES

IF THIS world seems too prosaic and you wish for one enlivened with elves, hobgoblins and errant spirits just tell your friends you are interested in psychic research. Surely your desire will be more than satisfied. Hardly a friend is absolutely bankrupt of strange experiences. At some time or other something has occurred that he feels, though does not admit, lies beyond the explanation of science.

More interesting than anything I have ever said in the talks which I have given on psychic research are the stories that my listeners gave me after the lectures. In this chapter I shall give you a sampling of the kind of tales that have been told to me. I shall give only those which came from the people whose word I should be willing to accept concerning the ordinary things in life.

A lady of about thirty-five years, a librarian in a university lost her husband through a violent death. Some nights after he had been buried he appeared standing at the foot of the bed. His appearance seemed quite natural. Remaining long enough for her to observe not only his features and their expression but his collar, tie and coat, she kept the vivid recollection of his appearance. The next morning her little boy who slept in the adjoining room came to her and said that he had seen his father standing by the bedside that night.

From a university professor comes this strange story. His sister was separated from her mother by many miles. The mother's brother was also some distance from his sister the night she died but both had a keen feeling that the one they loved was experiencing some tragedy, though they had no reason to believe her ill or dying.

Practically the same story was told me by a lady after one of my lectures recently. In this case it was a mother and sister who suddenly felt a deep concern for a brother and later learned of his death at approximately the time they had their distressing experiences.

After a lecture to a group of doctors who agreed with me that the bizarre happenings in spirit circles all find an explanation in natural science, several of them took me aside and started with the well known formula; "Doctor I know that you are right and I agree with your point of view but—" Among the stories they told me one stays clearly in mind. A number of American officers after the war were quartered in an old-fashioned house in the south of England. One night an orderly came tumbling down the steps and ran to his officer in a very obvious state of terror. His story was to the effect that as he turned the gas lights out on the third floor the face of a woman looked out at him from the wall. He was not enough of a soldier to stand that sort of a surprise attack. Moreover he swore that some one else would have to take over that detail. He would never turn lights out on the third floor any more. The officer inquired about his habits, especially the kind and amount of liquor he had been using. No banter or assurances could send that private to the third floor next evening. However, when his officer volunteered to accompany him, he went. Sure enough when the light went out the lady came in. Straight out from the wall she stared into their faces. Officer and man beat a retreat. Inquiries from some of the old people in the neighborhood brought out a story that ran back over a century. King George the Third had kept a beautiful mistress in this old home. He would occasionally come down and live with her. Then his ardor cooled and his visits became infrequent. Then the lady after months of weary loneliness ended her unhappy life with her own hand, but she never could free her spirit. Time and again through the century her unhappy eyes would look into those of men and women who walked the halls where she once had been so happy.

Here is another by a British officer. The scene is laid in Canada. Several young officers are quartered in a long stone house equipped with creaking stairs. This is what frequently happened. Those stairs would creak step by step from the bottom to the top. Then the hall floor boards would creak as though someone were softly stepping his way down to the last room at the end of the hall. Where my friend lodged, a beam of light from his room would cut across the hall between the head of the stairs and that end room. Whenever his door was open at night and the lamp burning the creaking steps and floor would register right up to that beam of light. Again and again my friend would jump out into the hall with his flash light and see exactly nothing.

Here is something similar with a better dénouement. A lady, two daughters and a son dwelt in Cambridge in the classic shades of old Harvard. Picture to yourself one of those quaint old American houses, built in what might be called the Carpenter's Age, with rooms of curious shape and stairways that seemed to be an afterthought of the builder. Such dry and seasoned wood is most hospitable to vagrant spirits. In this setting the mother of the lady departed this life and returned. On many occasions as the family sat in the library downstairs they would hear the planks of the front hall and the stairway respond to the slow step of an invisible visitor. They did not stop until they entered the room which had belonged to the elderly lady. In that room they could hear closet doors opening and closing and bureau drawers pulled out and thrust back. At first it was surprising and alarming, then it became amusing, and

then irritating. They did the correct thing for a
citizen of Cambridge. Calling in a Harvard professor they told him the story. He ventured an
experiment. A medium came and sat in the house
during the evenings. Finally, she declared that the
elderly lady's spirit had returned and was distressed
to learn that she had made so much noise. She
promised to come no more and claimed that she only
dropped in to see that things were tidied up. After
that she came no more. Only those who know the
New England housekeeper can really share her dis-
appointment.

This story really gets nowhere. Since it was told
to me by a psychologist for whom I have a great deal
of respect I shall enter it. Here the scene is a lonely
little house covered and surrounded with snow. In
the humble parlour stands a casket. My friend, then
a young man at college, is trying to comfort and help
the family. As the night wears on the members of
the family become very tired. He urges them to go
to bed and assures them that he will watch by the
casket during the night. After sitting in that lonely
room for some time he is violently startled by a
vigorous rattling at the door. Quickly swinging
it open he peers out into the night—deep blue sky
above and broad white wastes of snow beneath. Not
the mark of a footprint anywhere. Then his scientific curiosity is aroused. Out he goes and circles the
house. There is no sign of a footprint of man or

beast nor is the snow around the door disturbed. To this day he declares he has found no explanation.

I can think now of but one man who claimed to have come face to face with a veritable ghost. He was a sentinel in the German army during peace times. As he patrolled his beat his attention was attracted to a white figure coming down the road toward him. He was quite prepared to enjoy the joke of a fellow soldier and a sheet. However as it approached he did not like its gait. Seemingly it glided along without the bobbing motion of a person walking. As it approached him he noted that it was transparent. On its way past him, he reached out and touched it. Naïvely he remarked that it could not have come from hell as it was very cold and quite moist.

Of an altogether different character is the account I am about to give. This I have from Dr. Bull and it dates back to the time when I was working for the Society. Dr. Bull at that time was enjoying a very good but most unusual practice. He had been an intimate friend of Dr. Hyslop, the professor in Columbia University who had been led to accept the spiritistic hypothesis after a very thorough study of psychic phenomena. It seemed to Dr. Bull that if a Christian could believe his New Testament he could believe that some cases of apparent nervous or mental disorder are really due to demon possession. His treatment consisted in having a medium sit beside the patient who was in a relaxed and reclining position and endeavor to learn from the spirit world what sort of an evil spirit was causing his patient's troubles. Of the many interesting things he told me what I am about to tell impressed me most.

The doctor became acquainted with a man who had had practically no educational advantages, but who did some most remarkable things. At one time he felt that he was possessed by an ancient Aztec Indian. He showed me some of the work done by his patient. I recall some designs for the backs of playing cards. They were beautifully done. Anyone who had ever seen the art work of the Aztec could not fail to note its unique motifs running through the design. Then the doctor showed me another set of drawings done by his patient when held captive by the spirit of a designer. Here were some very pretty sketches of scroll work and some designs for screens. Then a third spirit visited this fortunate or unfortunate man and it was the spirit of a genius, a painter with imagination and technique. As a sample of this work the doctor had a large oil painting hanging on the wall. To me it seemed exquisitely done. It portrayed a sunset beyond a lake lying deep among towering mountains. One could see paths running along the mountainside and these the doctor told me had an allegorical significance. Follow one and it would lead you to the heights and out into the light, follow the other and you would be lost in the deep shadows of the mountains. So far as I could judge, it was a very good piece of art, in its colouring, in its symmetry and in the unity of its conception. Would not it be splendid if we could have the spirit of a genius visit us and enable us to do great things without the long years of tedious preparation?

Speaking of spirit possession suggests a story recently acquired. Let me give you a little preparation for this account. In order to write legibly it is necessary to train the muscles in the fingers of the right hand to make very small and precise movements. It is no easy task. Long hours are put in by little children in acquiring this feat. As the fingers obtain their dexterity a centre in the left hemisphere of the brain, for right-handed children, is slowly and elaborately educated. Before anyone can write, this development must be perfected. Now for the story: a little child about two years old whose tiny hands and fingers have the usual childish clumsiness, writes intelligent sentences, when the old folks are not in the nursery. Imagine it!

At the time when I collected that gem I obtained these two. In fact the story of the literary prodigy brought these two strange narratives · to mind. Again, perhaps a few words of explanation may give a setting for the stories.

From the most ancient times to the present there has been a widespread belief that discarnate spirits could enter into people and even into things. Among

the Babylonians and the Egyptians there are accounts of demon possession and methods by which
the evil spirits were driven out. Most of us are
acquainted with the incidents in the New Testament
where evil spirits came out at the word of command.
In the early Christian Era, the Church Fathers tell
us about cases of demon possession and the way in
which they were depossessed. In the Catholic Ency-
clopedia there is an interesting article on exorcism,
from which we learn that the present rite of exorcism
agrees with the teachings of the early Church Fathers
and is a proof of the continuity of Catholic tradition.
"According to Catholic belief demons or fallen angels
retain their natural power, as intelligent beings, of
acting on the material universe, and using material
objects and directing material forces for their own
wicked ends; and this power, which is in itself limited
and is subject of course to control of divine Provi-
dence, is believed to have been allowed a wider scope
for its activity in consequence of the sin of mankind.
Hence places and things as well as persons are naturally liable to diabolical infestation..." This of
course opens up interesting possibilities. Actual objects may be infested with malignant spirits and it
would be necessary to avoid using any such material
in the construction of churches. "The chief things
formally exorcised in blessings are water, salt and oil
and these in turn are used in personal exorcisms and
in blessing or consecrating places, (e.g. churches)

and objects (e.g. altars, sacred vessels, church bells) connected with public worship." In early times certain men were ordained to exorcise, though anyone who led a devout life and was a true believer could adjure the evil spirit to depart by the authority of a Higher Power.

Out in the wilds among a primitive people, a courageous priest is carrying out the duties of his calling. With a mind stored full of the wisdom and lore of the past he is trying to instil into the minds of those simple people the ideals and principles of Christianity. Among them he encounters one who speaks sentences in Greek. This is so foreign to the language and culture of these aborigines that the good priest assumes he has a case of spirit possession, similar to those which the church had known all through the ages. So he proceeded with his ritual to demand the departure of that linguistic demon.

In spiritualistic circles we sometimes hear of what is called a "poltergeist." This is a turbulent spirit. He raises the mischief when he enters the scene. I once knew a man who thought his father came back to earth as a "poltergeist." He would do very rude and uncouth things in the drawing-rooms of cultured spiritualists. Now it seems that for many years the Catholic Church has believed that inanimate things may be animated by wicked spirits and that it is possible to conjure them away.

So we have the setting for our second story. A

sweet and lovable nun lives in seclusion. To devote
her mind to holy meditation she makes little contact
with the outside world.   In such an atmosphere as
this comes the "poltergeist" or mischievous demon.
When her meals are brought to her, dishes rise up and
fling themselves on the floor, spoons and saucers
cavort around to the dismay and distress of everyone.
Again the ancient ritual, bearing with it memories
that run back through the Elizabethan Age, when
witches did their wicked work, back through the dark
Middle Ages, with their struggles against the powers
of darkness, back to the early Christians with the
hand outstretched, eyes uplifted and the holy words
of adjuration, comes into action in this scientific
twentieth century.

After those stories about the priests of the Catholic
church, one that I got from a Protestant pastor would
seem to be in order.   No starved ascetic was he but
a tremendous man of two hundred and forty pounds,
jolly, good-natured, and thoroughly practical.   At
some time in his life he acquired a conviction that he
could trust to his premonitions. Such things as
these would happen: as he coasted down a hill on his
bicycle he had a premonition that the chain was
about to jump off,—after a lapse of a few minutes
off came the chain.   Again he had a premonition that
one of the children would hurt his hand, and sure
enough the hand was hurt.   His most striking experience happened as follows.   With his two boys he

was hurrying to the station in Boston trying to catch a train for the West, when he pulled out his watch and discovered that the train had departed. Then there came to him a deep sense of relief and along with it a conviction that they had escaped some danger. He said to the boys that it was a good thing they had missed the train for he was sure that that train was going to meet with an accident. Several days later he happened to meet with one of the officials of that railroad and told him about missing, the train and the premonition of trouble. This led to a comparison of notes. And it evolved that the particular sleeper in which he and the boys had their reservation did meet with an accident. A freight train on a siding struck that car and ruined the berths he reserved. After this he had more confidence in his premonitions than ever and also he had more premonitions. Indeed, they became a nuisance; they beset him all the time. To test their real value he kept a close record of each premonition and what happened after. This cured him. He discovered that he had been taking account of only the few that came true. These were so striking that he forgot all about the others.

In sharp contrast with the genial and kindly clergyman are two gentlemen who made a precarious living following the races. This is their story. A lady they happened to know would go into a trance and see a race run in some distant city. She would see the track, horses and jockeys and the board on which the names of the horses were listed. There she would see the name of the winner before it was broadcast over the country. This advantage of a few minutes advance information netted some tidy sums to these gentlemen. Just what went on I could not discover. Certainly the lady seemed to make a number of lucky hits, but when she went into her "trance" and attempted to tell me what she saw my friend doing some forty miles away, her television apparatus was certainly out of order.

Even college professors with all their aversion for superstition occasionally run into a weird experience. One showed me a clever drawing of his house-front done by a friend who had never seen the house or had a description of it. Another told of an aunt who could gaze into a crystal ball and locate things that had been lost or misplaced.

Not all of these curious experiences are useless or impractical. A wealthy gentleman once told me that he had reason to believe that one of his relatives had put some valuable papers away very carefully before he died and had neglected to tell any one where they were put. Though he had been trained as a lawyer and was well versed in science he thought he would take a try with a medium. According to his account he obtained very specific directions to find the papers and found them, quite picturesquely, in an old trunk in an attic. Almost the same story was told me by a lady but in her case the papers were found in a library drawer.

If stories of this sort entertain you, get a few copies of the Proceedings of the English Society for Psychical Research. There you will certainly find some very striking and interesting things. Tell them to your friends and see what happens. I am sure that one friend out of three can tell you of some weird experiences that he has had.

CHAPTER VI

MEDIUMS IN GENERAL

WHEN I assumed my duties at the Society I began to look for raw material. Nothing can be done without dependable material. It seemed that no one in the Society knew of a single medium whom they could guarantee as honest and trustworthy. I suggested that we broadcast a letter among the membership and see what suggestions might arrive. This, I was told, was too dangerous a proceeding. Many members had their favorites and would insist upon a study of mediums who really had nothing to give. It appeared to be my job to get out into the highways and byways and discover some good material.

Taking one of the old magazines published by the Society I found an interesting account written by one of the officers of a sitting with a medium. This seemed to be a good beginning. I found the lady was a resident of New York and proceeded at once to a sitting. It was a hot summer night and a very charming little lady from the South cordially volunteered to give me some messages. I shall describe these in a later chapter. My interest was in the medium: whether her apparent trance was feigned, whether her replies were spontaneous, whether she was open to suggestions and would follow the lead made by my remarks or gestures. Certainly there was nothing in the situation to command my confidence and I left feeling that if this was a sample of what a high official considered an excellent medium, I had a hard time ahead of me finding any thing of interest.

The next experiment was with an English lady who volunteered the information that she had sat many times for a London society and had been accustomed to having a waiting list. It would appear that Londoners were much more interested in spiritualism than New Yorkers. She felt that we were a very mercenary and materialistic people. Her performance is rather typical of the usual medium. First, she had to assure me that she did not know whether she could make any communications or not. The powers that controlled her were entirely independent of her efforts. It was also made clear that if any spirit should begin speaking through her I should make a prompt reply. Spirits, it seems, are very sensitive and if one does not get *en rapport* with them readily they vanish. After these instructions she bound a dark cloth around her eyes, breathed heavily, sighed a few times and began to speak in what purported to be the broken English of an Indian maiden. Little Sunbeam undertook to act as a guide for some friends of mine in the spirit world. Detect-

ing my southern accent she furnished me with a
"Mammy." That was a fairly safe venture, but
unfortunately an English coloring entered the picture.
This robust matron was very plump, with shining red
cheeks. She exclaimed, "Do you remember when
you spilled your porridge?" Now that was just too
bad. Several negro mammies who ought to be in
heaven might remember my spilling many things, but
not an English porridge. After this episode I determined to have a little amusement for my two dollars.
Said the medium: "There is a Betty, or a Betsy
here." I sat silent for awhile, looked very serious
and then said in an awed voice, "Is Fred with her?"
This started quite a long explanation of how Fred
had gone over to the spirit land and had met Betsy
there. This apparently caused me a great deal of
surprise and distress. In a whisper I murmured,
"And the baby?" That touched off another explo-
sion. Betsy, Fred and the baby were presented in
a happy domestic scene. Fred, it seems, had improved his ways and could hardly be recognized as
the Fred who had behaved so badly on this planet.
Needless to say the three characters were fictions of
my imagination. Naturally, I could not make a very
enthusiastic report on this sitting.

Despite the fact that I found this Mrs. Anderson
quite impossible there were several members of the
Society who had known many mediums that declared
her a medium above the average in the interesting

and correct information that she gave. One very thorlligent and well educated lady was astonished and in teoughly convinced by what she heard.

Some sympathetic friends, seeing my despair, invited me to some group séances. In this type of séance the medium has a better opportunity to submit his messages. With a little ambiguity and ingenuity he can say something that must be significant to some one in the group. His messages come with much more promptness and certainty when he finds there are people in the circle who are sympathetic and responsive. Often he is led to switch from one hearer to another as someone in the circle exclaims that that message has a very pertinent meaning and must be intended for him. In none of these group séances could I discover anything that any clever person could not produce.

Finding New York in the summer of 1926 so very poorly supplied with good mediums I decided to go to Lily Dale, near Jamestown, in one of the most beautiful parts of the state of New York. Here mediums from all over the country come to a sort of a Chautauqua. They may be found by the score. Their signs appear in many windows as you walk down the cottaged streets. Thinking that seine fishing might net me something I decided to go right down one of the streets, visiting each medium who had his sign out.

Entering one of the little houses I was greeted by a

quaint, little, old Irish woman. She had no trouble
in working up a trance. One wrap of a long black
stocking around her eyes and she was ready to go.
She did not bother about working up her trance or
summoning an Indian spirit. She simply settled into
her chair and informed me that my father was there
and had a message for me. He had a great deal of
trouble making himself clear but the upshot of the
matter seemed to be that I ought to go out of the
brick business. By no exercise of my imagination
with symbolism or allegory could I connect this with
teaching psychology in Princeton. However, her
brogue was so delightful that I willingly received
messages from my sainted mother who was enjoying
a vacation at the seashore. This poor, old soul was
simply a humorous Irishwoman who was taking in
a few dollars in an easy way. She was quite typical
of the people on that street, but much more amusing.

At the hotel someone suggested that I visit a
medium whom Conan Doyle had highly recom-
mended. I easily found the young lady and read a
letter in her sitting room signed by Conan Doyle,
saying that this medium was of exceptional merit.
Naturally I was prepared for something of genuine
interest. True, she did have an interesting feature.
With her lips very slightly opened she could articulate
very clearly and distinctly. In fact it was very fas-
cinating to see her face so immobile and to hear her
voice apparently coming from deep in her throat.

A collar made it impossible for me to see any throat movements. Of course, the impression she sought to convey was that she was perfectly inert and that a spirit was speaking through her lips. The usual technique was evident. Quite frequently she would say, "Does this mean anything to you?" or she would interject, "Do you understand that?" The spirit claimed to have seen me in a uniform. I decided to help things along so I remarked, as though reminiscing, "That old Captain's uniform!" This was instantly productive of results. Curiously enough she promptly gave me the full name of a friend who had died. She informed me that he had died by my side in France. There was a slight discrepancy there as he was a professor in Princeton and had never been in the army. Keeping this to myself I readily agreed to his name and his demise. Thus encouraged, she marshalled a number of men, calling them by their first names and sketched some gory scenes in France. One could almost see the gun-flashes and smell the smoke. This was very diverting to me as I never got any nearer to France during the war than Mitchell Field, Long Island, and the only powder I ever smelt was on the cheeks of the girls in the canteen. Apparently Sir Arthur attracted a better grade of spirits.

All of this was very discouraging and I felt that I had made my trip in vain. However, there was one medium whom every one agreed was very remarkable. His name was Cartheuser. In this they were quite

correct. Getting acquainted with him well repaid
me for going to Lily Dale.

At the time of my visit there was a very clever
slate-writer by the name of Keeler, who attracted
a great deal of attention. When I visited him I had
on a golf suit and was in quite a cheerful frame of
mind. After scanning my face and figure closely
he said his powers would not work that morning and
that I need not return   That was an excellent lesson.
From that time on I dressed very soberly and wore
the mournful look of a man who wants to communicate with someone who has "gone before." This resulted in a much more cordial welcome among the
mediums.

Another star performer of those days was John
Slater. Apparently he would reach into a receptacle,
pull out an envelope in which a question had been
placed, read the question without opening the envelope, give an answer, then tear the envelope open,
scan its contents and toss it aside. He did this with
a great deal of assurance and very clearly impressed
large groups of people. Of course any one who has
read any works on magic knows several ways of
doing this sort of thing.

If you are interested in reading messages in sealed
envelopes to the mystification of your friends, a very
good procedure is this: supply some one in the group
with a single sheet of paper that just fits the envelope,
a soft black pencil and a needle and thread. The

instructions are, write your question on each side of the sheet, seal the envelope, run the thread through a number of times and tie the thread in a dozen knots. You then take the envelope, slip it in your pocket, where you have a sponge moistened with cologne. Get the cologne on one surface of the envelope. It then becomes transparent and the message can easily be read. I have found a number of people who wanted to impute psychic powers to me when I performed this feat.

On Sundays there would be a large gathering of people in the center of the place and some medium would give messages. Here we have much the same sort of thing that one finds in group séances. Speakers can always be confident that what they say will be true for someone in the audience.

It was my good fortune to sit next to one of the mediums who gave a long series of messages which were very well received. She was an elderly woman, robust, very normal in appearance and very sociable. Quite easily she drifted into conversation with me, told me about her life and family. From her early years she had felt an impulse to turn to anyone and to say whatever came to her lips. She claimed that she did not think over what she was about to say but simply spoke spontaneously whatever occurred to her. At times the impulse was much stronger and she had much more confidence than was her usual experience. I did not have the temerity to inquire why her messages were all so general and why she could not mention names or dates in the statements that came so positively from the dead.

Very frequently I am asked the question "Are there any honest mediums?" I should say there are quite a number of honest people who think that they are mediums. They have some very striking experiences. They do see faces that look out of the wall at them, or appear in the room before them. They often see figures standing beside the person. In addition to that many of them hear voices that give only a few words, leaving them to fill in the meaning. Some of them carry on conversations with these strange voices. Before psychiatry had collected and classified various cases of nervous disorders these phenomena were very perplexing. Now we know that there is a gland in the throat known as the "thyroid" and that it secretes into the blood stream. Chemical activity throughout the body is largely regulated by this gland. Physicians can tell whether it is secreting too much or too little. When it secretes too much we have a number of characteristic effects. Among these is a very much heightened imagination, which can result in just the sort of experiences described. I had an occasion to study such a case for two years. I found when the secretions of this gland were diminished that the patient lost the faculty for seeing faces and hearing voices.

We should not be too critical toward those who

have these vivid experiences and interpret them as spirit manifestations. It is a quite natural thing to do. I have a friend who does automatic writing, an educated and highly intelligent woman. Though she understands the psychological principle in automatic writing, her hand performs so independently of her thinking that she is often tempted to believe some other intelligence is directing the pencil. I venture to say that any normal man who saw quite clearly a head looking out of the wall would be led to think that there really was a head there. We all have ways of checking up on illusions and mistakes of perception that we make and we can tell pretty well what is due to our fancies and what is due to facts. Let something come into our experiences which seems to come as an actuality and we are very prone to accept it as such.

Many people in private life admit that they are mediums and occasionally see a figure that speaks a message. As they have no mercenary motive and as they often seem embarrassed by their experience, we certainly must conclude that they are not frauds. If one really is determined to study mediums this would seem to be the best class of people to study. Unfortunately they are not easy to find. They are rather sensitive and not particularly keen about scientific studies.

There is one thing that characterizes every medium, the *trance*. Great or insignificant, remarkable

or awful, one and all they must have a trance. From
a very light trance, hardly detectable, to a condition
of complete helplessness, these mystic states will
range. Some mediums emphasize their trance.
Others put little interest in it; apparently they are
not changed conspicuously by the condition that
allows a discarnate spirit to take possession of their
speech centers! Naturally, among the thinking
mediums quite a little is made of their trance condition. To emphasize the fact that what they are saying cannot come from their own minds they will have
various stories to tell about the peculiar condition
into which they lapse. One assured me that he
would lapse into a trance while asleep and wake up
to find himself sprawling on the floor. Another told
me that her trance was very light and that she spoke
her messages somewhat as an ordinary person speaks
without thinking of what they are saying.

Trances appealed to me. Here was something
that I knew a little about, for I had some experience
with the hypnotic trance and had on numerous occasions observed the so-called trances incident to some
mental disorders. If there were such a thing as a
medium trance it seemed to me that it might resemble
the kind of a condition that we find in hypnosis. Let
us make some comparisons.

In order to get a person to go into a hypnotic
trance for the first time the usual procedure is to
seat him comfortably, and get his confidence and

coöperation. Suggest to him that he cannot lower his upraised hand. Repeat this a number of times. Then tell him to try to lower his hand. He cannot do it. Often this simple experiment is successful. Nevertheless I have seen a professional hypnotist work for twenty minutes with a medical student who wished to be hypnotized, but without any success. Now the only point I wish to make here is that no one simply drops into the hypnotic trance as a natural or common experience. It is artificial and induced.

On the other hand, the mediums who have discussed the matter with me suggested that their trances were something supernormal and that they had come without the aid of any other person. From their descriptions it would seem that they had some peculiar trait, different from that other mortals possessed, and the trance came easily ·and naturally to them. Certainly they claimed to drop off into a trance at any time convenient for them. Only after being hypnotized many times can a subject hypnotize himself. Such subjects will occasionally go into a trance involuntarily. Perhaps they have been hypnotized frequently with the aid of some bright shiny object. Sudden appearances of bright shiny objects will occasionally throw them into the trance. Never have I heard of a medium who had any troubles of this sort.

To get a subject out of a deep trance it is often necessary to suggest to him that he is waking up.

You can note by his breathing how he slowly comes out of the hypnotic state. Never shall I forget the first man whom I hypnotized. So deep did he go that I could not wake him by clapping my hands or shouting in his ear. It was an awful moment. Probably several minutes were spent in trying to bring him out. Contrast this with the way in which a medium snaps out of what is apparently a state of coma. He may be lolling in his chair, an inert figure breathing very deeply, but a suspicious movement of a sitter will bring him out with startling rapidity.

It has not been my good fortune to find mediums who would allow me to experiment with their trance states. One, however, I shall never forget. She had fascinated some devotees of the race track. Her forte was to go into a trance and to see what horses were winning on distant tracks. Her advance information seemed to pay better than the usual "dope sheets." Voluntarily she undertook to go into her trance and tell me what a friend was doing in a distant city. I seated her by a window and told her that the room was dark and then turned her head to the bright side of the room to see if my suggestion affected her iris reflex. It did not. Possibley I should not mention this as the conditions were all very poor and neither my suggestion nor the light might have been adequate to prevent the reflex.

There are numerous ways of determining whether

a person is really in the hypnotic trance and subject
to the will of another person. Suggestions which
make a person do things that he cannot do of his own
volition are the best evidence. Thus I have seen a
boy told that he was in the sun on a hot day and he
broke out in a perspiration. Another youngster was
told that the lobe of his ear was very cold and that
there was no blood in it. When a needle was thrust
through the lobe not a drop of blood exuded. These
are rather drastic measures. However, the medium
who insists that his body and brain are at the disposal
of some vigorous spirit and compares his condition
to that of a subject controlled by a hypnotist should
be willing and should be able to prove it by just such
tests.

Comparing the ostensible trances of mediums with
those of hypnotized persons there are some rather
obvious differences.   In hypnosis the subject is often
responsive to just one person, refusing to take directions from anyone except the person who has put him
under. Others may shout and command all to no
purpose. Mediums, however, slip from the direction
of one spirit to another. Moreover the hypnotist
can make various portions of his subject's skin in-
sensitive, or can throw him into a catatonic state with
ease. Never have I seen any spirit attempt such a
thing with a medium, though I have known one medium who claimed that she was completely at the

disposal of the spirit who possessed her and maintained that she was in a state quite similar to the hypnotic state.

So far as my observations are concerned I must say that the mediums whom I have observed do not seem to resemble, in their trances, any of the genuine trances I have been able to study with hypnotic subjects or nervous patients.

Many of the rules of the séance are very amusing. One is that a group of sitters shall arrange themselves in a circle and join hands. In addition to this they should keep both feet resting on the floor. By way of explanation, the medium points out that the power which is to produce the phenomena is something like electricity. Hence it is necessary to complete the circuit and let the power flow from person to person. Inasmuch as electrical currents often have to be grounded the feet must rest upon the floor. If you have sat in such a circle you must have noticed that you cannot do much exploring with your hands and feet kept in such positions. Never did I realize the value of grounding the current so strongly as on one eventful night. Tired and bored with a séance that was dragging, I had tilted my chair back and crossed my knees. The tip of my toe came in contact with the medium who was crawling about the circle.

Another rule is that there must be music or songs. Most amazing is the explanation for this. We are told that psychic power comes in vibrations, resembling the Hertzian waves that play our radios. To catch these waves we must have waves in the air of the room. To prove this the phenomena often occur when the songs are loudest. Such a little discrepancy as the fact that the radio waves travel in the ether and the sound waves travel in the air does not bother the spiritualist. Again I learned to appreciate the value of this rule when I conducted a séance of my own. If you have to leave your seat and fix a few gadgets the "Battle Hymn of the Republic" is an invaluable friend to cover any noises that you have to make.

Good mediums are artists in timing their phenomena. Things happen when the sitter's attention is directed to a lively conversation or engrossed in trying to remember and sing a hymn. I did not dare to show an apparition in my séance at any other time than the moments when my group was somewhat preoccupied. A circle of people all intent and alert to observe what a medium is doing will kill any séance.

Darkness is an indispensable requirement in many séances. Sometimes the dark is not complete. Nothing is more difficult than to shut out every little leak of light. So a partial darkness where one can dimly see the outlines of other sitters is sometimes quite sufficient. Occasionally mediums insist upon absolute darkness. Then the blackness is so complete you can pass your hand before your eyes and detect no difference in the darkness. Explanations for this requirement are about as follows. Psychic forces are akin to light but not so strong and the light destroys them. Dr. Crandon, the husband of the famous medium Margery, declared that it was as absurd to expect psychic phenomena in a strong light as to expect that you could develop a sensitive photographic plate with the sun shining on it. He maintained that there is a law governing the psychic phenomena and we must conform to it if we are to have results. This, he claimed, is a demand no more unreasonable than what is imposed upon us in all branches of science.

One cannot help thinking that, if it is possible for a spirit or a group of vibrations to take possession of a medium who delivers messages in a well lighted room, it or they really need not operate in the dark. Scepticism of these psychic laws increases when we note that the movement of trumpets and the touches of spirit hands only occur in deep darkness.

Darkness certainly has a valuable psychological effect for the spiritualist. Many people become nervous and apprehensive in the dark. Once I sat next to a Chicago business man who seemed to have a great deal of poise and confidence before the lights went out, but when the darkness fell his assurance dropped. The hand that held mine shook as though he had paralysis agitans. On another occasion a rather nervous lady about rubbed the skin off of my knuckles as she twisted her ringed fingers around mine. Indeed, some people have such a fear of the dark that they are in no frame of mind to understand what is going on about them. In one pitch black room I have known a young college girl to become so excited that she thought she was going into a trance and had to be taken out.

Some very clever work and very puzzling can be done by a good medium in the dark. I have had my eyebrow gently stroked by a medium who was so alert that when I thrust my head forward to reach his hand it was gone. Really it is quite disconcerting to sit in an absolutely dark room and feel a pair of cold clammy fingers pinch your ear. I must admit that the precision of these movements in the dark puzzled me for some time. When a trumpet can touch you lightly on the edge of your eyeglass and then move deftly away you cannot help feeling that someone who can see in the dark is moving that trumpet. But you know no one can see in the dark. When there is no light to be focussed no human nor animal eye can see. Quite a few of my very sceptical and critical friends confess their puzzlement about these experiences. My first insight into how they were done was supplied by Mrs. Houdini, who told me that such a knack can be acquired by anyone who will take the trouble to experiment in the dark. Of course you cannot see; but, with a little practice, you can locate a person very nicely by the sound of their breathing. Then if you are determined to become an artist in this sort of thing you can by constant practice determine where your sitter is and where his ears and nose can be found without fumbling. I found that by putting a medium's trumpet to my ear I could locate a sitter quite nicely, as it caught the faint sounds of his breathing and indicated his position by the direction it pointed.

Assuming that some mediums are honest and genuine it would be interesting to compare them with normal human beings. Many studies have been made of the inheritance of insanity, genius and special talents. Taking my cue from this I made it a practice to ask each medium if there were any members of his family who had "psychic powers." I was frequently told that a parent, grandparent, aunt or uncle had some such power. I cannot say that there is anything conclusive in this little investigation. It is merely suggestive. Everyone knows how difficult it is for social workers to get adequate information about several generations of any family. In my cases I was dealing with people who were certainly not very dependable. Some of them may have felt that their own abilities would be enhanced in my opinion if they came from a family of psychics. However, I did carry away the impression that some of the more frank and sincere mediums were telling the truth and doing so intelligently. If it should prove to be true that the ability to see visions and hear messages is hereditary, it would seem to indicate that conditions in the thyroid gland may be of an hereditary character.

CHAPTER VII

CAN SPIRITS GO CRAZY?

WHEN I first began reading stenographic notes of what mediums had said I had a curious feeling. Though I had not seen a medium for twenty years and had no idea of how they expressed themselves when I began my work for the Society, I found that there was something strikingly familiar in the character of the messages I read. At first I could not quite recall what experiences could give rise to this feeling of familiarity that I had in reading stenographic reports of a séance. Then it suddenly dawned on me. These disconnected ideas and strange twisting and turning of the attention from one notion to another was just the thing that one noticed with a number of mental patients. When a case of schizophrenia is communicative and has not reached too advanced a stage of dementia, one hears just the sort of thing that many a medium gives. Here is a sample of the statements of a medium who was acceptable to so experienced a connoiseur as Dr. Bull.

105

At Dr. Bull's office

October 7, 1926
2.45 P.M.

Present: Mrs. D. (Medium), Dr. McComas, Dr. Bull, and Recorder.

Mrs. D. (Impressions—Long pause). Very many impressions are flowing in, but rather crossed at the moment. As I first shook hands with the gentleman a little lady of unusual sweetness manifested, with the remark "A lady of fifty years ago." I didn't see her in vision, but knew she was small, and that although very kind, sweet and gentle in her dealings, that underneath it were the foundations of character and a firm faith in God, that nothing could shake. She didn't hesitate to speak her mind in the same gentle way, but decidedly, where matters of principle were concerned. As I stepped into the room and sat down, I was flashed an Indian of the early type in America. When I asked why, the answer was that the ancestors of the gentleman were almost as much entitled to American claim as the force. I don't get on which side. The next indistinct impression was a man saying, "If I offer you an olive branch, will that connect as a slight cross-reference to something I previously said?" Now that was a little indistinct, and I would rather go into it a little deeper. (Turns away from light and covers eyes) A man a little heavier-set than the Professor, and possibly slightly shorter, dressed in black, with clothes that show, across the abdomen, a loss of weight, who was troubled with his breathing and says: "Son, I am trying to keep my word, my promise." Whether this is in relationship I do not know. I go now to a study. I am attempting to compile something and at times, take out volumes quite bulky. As I enter into this as a vibration, my back tingles, and all down my arms; and with it also comes a heaviness with my head. At times everything moves rapidly in this work, and with amazingly clear glimpses, and insights which I almost feel are all my own. At other times this heaviness comes over me and I am unable to concentrate and continue with the work. I work in two different lines, one in which I am supposed to be more competent to work and express myself. In the other I feel unworthy, and yet impelled by a sense of both duty and an urge; a duty to three people to do justice to these people. I have read extensively of records, both published and unpublished; some concerning a man whom I knew, and others concerning a man whom I did not know in life but whom I admire; and wish to carry on in whatever way I may be able to help. As one nears the meridian of life one is not so much concerned of devoting himself to a work that, to certain people, lacks scientific standards. In the thirties such things loom big; but around fifty—I hear fifty-six but am not sure—one is more interested in the vital meaning of life itself; not, as our opponents think, because one foot is slipping. A change of control. It is J. H.

Compare that with the following stenographic report from a patient at the Sheppard-Enoch Pratt Hospital kindly loaned me by Dr. G. Wilson Shaffer.

"There is something interesting going on here. A little girl over in the Casino reminds me of some Syrians I knew in California. One of these did a carving in mother-of-pearl of the 'Last Supper.' Any one interested in this type of girl would remind me of these people. The mothers of these Syrian rug dealers would adopt these girls and try to find their relatives. These vibrations are not entirely clear. There are vibrations in the room all the time. I do not know the purpose or where they come from. That girl interests me and reminds me of these Syrian men. The vibrations have annoyed a number of people in Atlanta also. The floors at home echoed

when I walked on them and they do sometimes here. The
vibration sounds seem to work around one. I don't hear
definite voices, they just work around me. For instance, in
Harper's Bazaar there is a picture of Eva La Gallienne. This
business has gone on for six months. Sister had to move twice
because of it. I think father's money had something to do
with it. There is that picture of the negress kneeling beside a
bed. I have seen my sister's maid kneel that way. I think
it was her—she said at that time there were——what about
that negro woman and the white mistress. The words do not
matter, it is the tone of voice. What about the woman who
had an affair with her negro chauffeur. They trained a big
bird to fly out at the chauffeur. I don't see why they said
that about my chauffeur. My sister fell in love with her Irish
chauffeur and wanted to marry him. The newspapers and
charitable organizations have something to do with it. This
has nothing to do with a *chaise lounge* or *affaire de coeur*.
I have heard that for six months through vibrations. The
vibrations come from across the way by means of a music box.
The words are translated to me and ask 'how old are you?'
Have you had your breakfast? They come in layers through
atmosphere charged with electricity. Two types of people are
constantly going in and out, the 'guinea pig' and the 'monkey
type.' All of the larger cities in the country are having trouble
with people copying other people's writing. I haven't written
a thing in three years—everything is printed. I would rather
go to Atlanta and hear the vibrations than not be able to attend
to my affairs. I know they are operating on patients downstairs without narcotics. I know my mother is downstairs.
My baby is on some ward being tortured. The Russians are
responsible. The 'impressions' say that a Russian nobleman
is the cause of it all. There are poisonous and gaseous fumes
about here. The lost steel plates are important to both the
German Government and the U. S. International peace is

dependent upon their recovery. They must be returned to the Metropolitan Museum. The Dresden china bowl was important to this country. It is a gift from the German Government. There will be a serious airplane disaster shortly—five Italian Naval officers will be killed—the Japanese government is responsible. Ether waves are spreading disgrace through my family."

One of three conclusions may be drawn from the character of messages of this type. First, the medium may be cleverly casting about touching upon all sorts of topics in the hope of catching her hearer's interest. Second, the medium may lapse into a reverie and allow all sorts of disconnected things to run through her mind. If she is hyperthyroid she may see faces and hear voices which will accentuate her peculiarities. Third, if the spiritualist is right, the visiting spirit has clearly gone crazy.

CHAPTER VIII

A DE LUXE CASE

NEARLY all the interesting cases that appear in the literature have to do with people in a rather lowly station in life with little education and frequently very stupid. Moreover, it has always seemed just about impossible to make good and continuous observations of what they said and did. As a result we have a great mass of reports that really get nowhere. Imagine then the delight of everyone interested in psychic research the world over when a surgeon in Boston announced to the world that his wife was a genuine psychic. At last there had come the great occasion that everyone directly or remotely interested in psychic phenomena had long desired. Now it seemed that the scientific world could really get an insight into the curious things that men like Crookes, Lodge, Richet and James had been writing about; for surely a man who boasted descent from the passengers on the Mayflower, who graduated from Harvard, who had the Harvard medical degree and was an instructor in surgery in that university for a number of years could be counted upon to take and maintain a really scientific attitude. No other rôle could be played by a man who was known as the

110

author of a book on surgical after-treatment, who was
a consulting surgeon for several hospitals and a Fellow of the American College of Surgeons. So it
seemed.

After I had had a few conversations with several
of the leading members in the Society this Boston
case was described to me. I had known something of
it from newspaper articles. The *Scientific American*
had offered a prize to anyone who could exhibit some
psychic phenomena which could not be explained in
terms of principles which were already known. Dr.
Crandon entered his wife as a candidate and a very
dignified group of men acted as judges: William
McDougall, Professor of Psychology at Harvard,
D. F. Comstock, of the Massachusetts Institute of
Technology, H. Houdini, the famous magician, W. F.
Prince, then Research Officer of The American Society for Psychical Research, Mr. Hereward Carrington, author of books on spiritualism, and a Mr. J. M.
Bird, who acted as secretary to this committee.
What really impressed the public was that some of
the men whose judgment was respected felt that they
could not declare themselves and that they were
frankly puzzled. That Houdini should declare
against the genuineness of the phenomena was not
surprising. That Carrington and Bird should be
favorably impressed was not surprising. That men
like McDougall, Comstock and Prince should be puzzled and wish for a further investigation was indeed

interesting.   It was the uncertainty of these men that
led to wide publicity for the case and attracted a
number of people to the famous little house at Number 10 Lime Street.   Articles appeared from time to
time in the newspapers and magazines and an interesting book was written by Bird describing the
strange happenings in the doctor's home.

In Conan Doyle's *History of Spiritualism* he speaks
with enthusiasm of Mrs. Crandon.

"No account of physical mediumship would be complete
which did not allude to the remarkable results obtained by
'Margery,' the name adopted for public purposes by Mrs.
Crandon, the beautiful and gifted wife of one of the first surgeons in Boston.   The lady showed psychic powers some years
ago, and the author was instrumental in calling the attention
of *The Scientific American* Committee to her case.   By doing
so he most unwillingly exposed her to much trouble and worry
which were borne with extraordinary patience by her husband
and herself.   It was difficult to say which was the more annoy-
ing, Houdini, the conjurer, with his preposterous and ignorant
theories of fraud, or such 'scientific' sitters as Professor Mac-
Dougall of Harvard, who after fifty sittings and signing as
many papers at the end of each sitting to endorse the wonders
recorded, was still unable to give any definite judgment, and
contented himself with vague innuendos.   The matter was not
mended by the interposition of Mr. E. J. Dingwall, of the
London S. P. R., who proclaimed the truth of the mediumship
in enthusiastic private letters, but denied his conviction at
public meetings.   These so-called 'experts' came out of the
matter with little credit, but more than two hundred common-
sense sitters had wit enough and honesty enough to testify
truly as to what occurred before their eyes.   The author may

add that he has himself sat with Mrs. Crandon and has satisfied himself, so far as one sitting could do so, as to the truth and range of her powers." (A. C. Doyle, *The History of Spiritualism*, Vol. 2, pp. 219–220.)

From this quotation it is easily seen what bitterness grew up among those who endorsed Margery toward those who could not agree with them.

In another place in his history Sir Arthur Conan Doyle, M.D., LI.D., expresses himself even more vigorously.

"What may be called a collective investigation of a medium, Mrs. Crandon, the wife of a doctor in Boston, was undertaken in the years 1923–1925 by a committee chosen by *The Scientific American* and afterwards by a small committee of Harvard men, with Dr. Shapley, the astronomer, at their head. It may be briefly stated that of *The Scientific American* inquirers the secretary, Mr. Malcolm Bird, and Dr. Hereward Carrington announced their complete conversion. The others gave no clear decision which involved the humiliating admission that after numerous sittings under their own conditions and in the presence of constant phenomena, they could not tell whether they were being cheated or not. The defect of the committee was that no experienced spiritualist who was familiar with psychic conditions was upon it. Dr. Prince was very deaf, while Dr. MacDougall was in a position where his whole academic career would obviously be endangered by the acceptance of an unpopular explanation. The same remark applies to Dr. Shapley's committee, which was all composed of budding scientists. Without imputing conscious mental dishonesty, there is a sub-conscious drag towards the course of safety. Reading the report of these gentlemen with their signed acquiescence at each sitting with the result, and their final verdict of fraud, one cannot discover any normal way in which they have reached their conclusions. On the other hand, the endorsements of the mediumship by folk who had no personal reasons for extreme caution were frequent and enthusiastic. Dr. Mark Richardson, of Boston, reported that he had sat more than three hundred times, and had no doubt at all about the results. The author has seen numerous photographs of the ectoplasmic flow from 'Margery,' and has no hesitation, on comparing it with similar photographs taken in Europe, in saying that it is unquestionably genuine, and that the future will justify the medium against her unreasonable critics." (A. C. Doyle, *History of Spiritualism*, Vol. 1, pp. 328–329.)

So said Conan Doyle.   One wonders what Sherlock Holmes would have said.

Indeed, the case of Margery loomed so large in spiritualist circles that it dominated everything else. Everywhere in psychic research literature one found Margery the outstanding character.   At the American Society for Psychical Research it was frequently said that Margery was the climax. With her the case for spiritualism would be won or lost.   Enthusiastic believers quoted her séances with conviction. All that was needed they felt was a fair, scientific investigation and the cause of spiritualism would be established for all time.   On the other hand, if it was proven that Margery's phenomena were done by trickery, psychic research would receive a blow from which it would never recover.   So said one of the oldest members to me.

Those who are interested in a detailed account of the origin and development of the Margery case up to 1925 will find the book entitled *Margery* by J. Malcolm Bird very interesting. It is written from the point of view of one who believed in the spiritistic hypothesis. It is written in a style to give the impression that the observations are critically and scientifically made and that the evidence was so great that one was forced to the belief that trickery must be ruled out, at least in a number of important instances.

We are not interested to review all the literature on the Margery case, the attacks and the defense. Here is presented only my own experiences and impressions.

At the Society I met two very able lawyers, men whose judgment any one could respect. In careful and guarded statements they described to me their impressions of the Crandons and what was going on at Number 10 Lime Street. Naturally I was very keen to get to Boston as soon as possible. Very kindly they made arrangements and I obtained my entreé to the famous séances.

At that time a typical séance was about as follows. One was taken to the fourth floor and shown the room where the séances were held. On one side stood a large glass cabinet of sufficient size to enable Mrs. Crandon to be seated comfortably within it. Small windows were cut through the walls at a convenient height so her hands could be thrust through and any-one who wished could satisfy themselves that her hands were in the positions where they had been fastened at the beginning of the séance. Staples were placed in the floor and her feet were securely fastened to them. When the door was closed the medium was shut off from the circle except by way of the two exposed hands.

Another cabinet made of cloth over a secure framework was opened on one side only. This enabled the medium to make contact with the circle and also with a small table which was placed in front of the cabinet.

Other objects of interest to the visitor were a small "bell-box" and an elaborate "voice cut-out." The bell-box was simply constructed and contained dry-cell batteries and a little electric bell. The box could be closed tightly and a flap hinged to the top could be pressed down against a spring until two contacts came together, which rang the bell. It was all very simple and a high school boy could easily understand it. The voice cut-out was more complicated. It consisted of a long glass tube bent in the shape of the letter U, which stood in an upright position. It was half filled with water and two corks floated on the surface of the water in each arm of the tube. The corks were painted with luminous paint so they could be seen in the dark. Attached to one arm of the U-tube was a heavy rubber tube, so constructed that it could not be squeezed to prevent the passage of air.

When one blew through the rubber tube the water went down in one arm of the U-tube and up in the other. In the dark you could easily see the two corks move from a position where they were side by side to one in which one cork was much higher than the other. As long as one continued to blow against the water column the corks would maintain their uneven position. Instead of holding the end of the rubber tube in the mouth a glass mouthpiece, fitted on the tube, was held in the mouth. This was built with three openings. Each lip covered an opening and the tongue covered the third opening. If either lip or the tongue slipped from their openings air would enter the tube and the corks would drop back to their even position. Thus in the dark one could see whether the person whose voice was being controlled moved the tongue or lips.

Visitors were encouraged to examine the cabinets and to experiment with the bell-box and voice cut-out. They were invited to explore the room and to satisfy themselves that there were no trick gadgets concealed anywhere.

At séances where there were critical visitors Margery was stripped before entering the séance room and searched to make sure that she had no reaching rod or other device concealed on her. Then led by two investigators she would be brought to the glass cabinet and her hands and feet lashed with picture wire which was securely fastened to prevent slipping.

After she was comfortably seated a small basket which had been daubed with luminous paint was placed between her feet in the cabinet. Spectators could easily see the spots of luminous paint on the basket, though everything else was completely invisible in the dark. After a few minutes the lights could be seen to rise, sway back and forth, and then go flying into the back of the cabinet. It was claimed that this was done by ectoplasm, which came from the medium's person and exuded from some orifice, ear, nose, mouth, etc. Then the door was opened and a small container was placed before the medium holding a number of carved wooden letters. These would be tossed out to the sitters in the circle. A hoarse whisper could be heard coming from the cabinet which would say, for example, "Here is an M for you, Dr. Mac." And I would find a little wooden M by my feet.

More impressive than the basket and the letters was the voice cut-out. It was placed before the medium and the nipple inserted in her mouth. Then the corks would change position, showing that she had blown into the tube and was holding her lips and tongue stationary. During this time "Walter" would indulge in some remarks, possibly he would carry on a conversation with sitters in the circle.

After these performances in the closed cabinet the medium would take her seat in the open cabinet. Before her on a small table the bell-box would be placed. Sitters were distributed in a circle around the table and would often be called upon to "control" the medium and each other. Such a control often consisted of someone's sitting next to Margery holding her hand and keeping one foot upon one of her feet. Then hands were joined around the circle reaching to the sitter on the other side of Margery who maintained a similar "control." Frequently no such procedure was followed and all hands and feet were free.

While the medium was in the open cabinet a sitter would often ask "Walter" to ring two shorts and one long with the box, or any signal which occurred to mind. Promptly the bell-box responded with the signal requested. This was done many times to the delight and bewilderment of the sitters. Then Walter would say "Turn on the red light, pick up the box, carry it over to the light, turn around to show there are no strings tied to it and bring it quickly back to the table and I will make it ring all the time it is off the table." This performance usually went forward just as Walter predicted.

With this same arrangement of medium and sitters Walter did one of his most choice acts. So convincing was this performance that one of the leading lawyers in New York and a professor of philosophy from Princeton declared that it was the nearest approach to something supernormal they had ever encountered and they were somewhat inclined to think that only the spiritistic hypothesis could explain it. It consisted in drawing a card from a pack which had not been opened until taken into the dark room and tossing it on the table without knowing what it was, whereupon Walter would tell them what the card was and to remember what he had said. When the light was turned on each card would be found named correctly. To introduce a little innovation the professor of philosophy wrote on one of the cards with a blue pencil and Walter told him what was written. All of this was done very promptly in a room which was absolutely dark. Walter's explanation was that he felt the cards with his ectoplasmic rod.

Once in a while this arrangement of sitters and cabinet was used to experiment with the ectoplasm: A plaque made luminous with a little luminous paint would be placed on the table and a dark object could be seen protruding over the plaque coming from the direction of the medium.

All that is just a sketch of an evening with Margery. In fact it is nothing more than the outlines of a sketch. It does not carry any good portrayal of a séance. To get that it is necessary to fill in and make a more complete picture. Imagine yourself invited to one of Dr. Crandon's evenings, including an invitation to dinner. Down in an old historic section of Boston you would find his house, suggesting memories of many historic things that occurred in Boston. After the quaint little Japanese butler admitted you to a charming parlor you would find yourself face to face with a handsome, middle-aged surgeon who knew the secret of hospitality and put you quickly at ease. Something about the pleasant expression in his blue-gray eyes that looked so clearly and honestly in yours would suggest to you other men of his profession of character and ability. If you had come prepared to be critical and hostile you would find it hard to keep that attitude towards so charming a gentleman.

When Mrs. Crandon was presented she would completely upset all preconceptions of the famous medium. A very attractive blonde with a charming expression and excellent figure the "Witch of Lime Street" proved to be a thoroughly feminine lady with the best traits of a mother and housekeeper. Her vivacity, with the doctor's poise and dignity, made them a delightful pair for an enjoyable dinner. Both had a very diverting sense of humor and the conversation would never lag.

After the meal, which frequently involved a little wine that warmed your heart, you would be invited into the library. There the atmosphere was that of literary Boston—comfortable chairs, books everywhere. Probably the doctor would call you aside and tell you that he wished to show you some interesting photographs. As he showed you some excellent pictures of his wife with "ectoplasm" coming from her ear or nose he might tell you something of the curious things which had been happening in his home. With a quiet, well-modulated voice he might tell you how the mediumship started a few years before in a simple experiment with table tipping. Then he might go on explaining how the table would rap out answers to questions. Several spirits seemed to be present, among them Walter Stinson, his wife's brother, who had been killed in a railroad accident about fifteen years before. Gradually Walter dominated the evenings. After some experiments he succeeded in taking possession of his sister. He would not use her voice but managed a device of his own which was apparently attached to the side of his sister's head, as the "voice cut-out" made speech by Mrs. Crandon impossible. If all of this impressed you sufficiently the doctor might continue by telling you of such strange things as these:

When a basin of liquid paraffine had been put in the séance room they would occasionally find a perfect paraffine glove, as though someone had thrust a hand into the paraffine, and drawn it out with a thin coating over it and the wrist. No human hand could be slipped out of such a glove without tearing the wrist. Only a hand that is at one time material and at another immaterial could make such a glove! On another occasion they put a chemical scale in the room, weighted one pan and found that the other pan, though empty, would be thrust down lifting up the weighted pan. On another occasion Margery wrote quite sensible sentences in languages she did not understand. When all of these experiments had been carefully explained by the doctor he would probably add that he was delighted to have you share his interest and would be more than delighted if you could offer some explanation of them.

Probably while the doctor was talking with you some of his friends would drop in for the séance of the evening. You might meet Dr. Mark A. Richardson, who had some reputation for work he had done on typhoid vaccination. You could not fail to like him. A representative of New England's best ideals would be the impression he would give you. Certainly you would not be led by what you knew of his career or by his manner and conversation to think of him as a magician's assistant. Nor would his wife give rise to any such idea. Certainly the portly and genial old gentleman they would present as Judge Hill would seem the very antithesis of a master of tricks. Also a Dr. Brown would add to the general impression that you were in a company of intelligent and responsible people. Perhaps if you met Mr. Dudley you might think him a little too reticent, but if you engaged him in conversation you would soon see that he had the scientific training and point of view.

After this social hour you would find yourself going with this interesting group up to the séance room. However, you might feel about ghosts and goblins you certainly would feel that you were in for a divert-

ing evening.   In the dark room you would meet the
most intriguing personality of all.   True, he would be
only a husky whisper.   But what he could whisper!
The most curious twists and turns ran into his dia-
logues.   When my full name was given, with the
middle name of Clay, Walter promptly exclaimed,
"No, I am clay."   Few people ever dared to engage
in an exchange of wits with Walter.   Just as the
Elsie voice built up into a personality with Cartheuser, so did Walter at Lime Street.

As you would leave late in the evening after saying
good-bye to your new and interesting friends, you
would probably find your thoughts taking one of two
directions.   If you had felt kindly toward the spiritistic interpretation of the things you had read about
in psychic research you would probably say to yourself: "This is the best argument for my belief that I
have ever found."   If, on the other hand, your training and habits of thinking made spiritualism impossible you would say to yourself: "What under the
sun are these people up to?   Are they planning to
make a grand exposé of the spiritualists by presenting
the greatest show of all and then explaining it?   Maybe they are just having some fun, for the evening
was full of amusing incidents,—could that be it?"

Such questions as these were undoubtedly in the
minds of the officers of the American Society for
Psychical Research, for they were anxious to have a
committee to study the Margery case fully and fairly.

They felt that the preceding investigations had not led to definite conclusions. So I was assigned the task of making up such a committee. After several conferences I succeeded in getting Professor Knight Dunlap of the Johns Hopkins University and Professor Robert W. Wood of the same university to agree to serve with me. Professor Dunlap is one of the outstanding psychologists in America with a genius for experimental work which is second to none, a man of many interests and the author of numerous well-known books in his science. Professor Wood is one of the greatest physicists in America. His brilliant experiments in electricity and light have given him an international reputation. Like his colleague, Professor Dunlap, his interests and activities reach out beyond his science. It would have been impossible to find two men famous in the scientific world better adapted for this sort of an investigation. The Society saw this at once and the Commission was appointed.

After a conference with Dr. Crandon an agreement was made to the effect that the sittings should take place in Boston, subject to cancellations "when the psychic's health makes it necessary." Dictated notes were to be taken during each séance of what was being observed, or of any comments. "Claims or suggestions of fraud in the production of phenomena which do not appear in these notes shall be deemed excluded from consideration." Dr. Crandon, Dr.

Richardson or some other physician was to be present as a medical attendant to the psychic. No "psychic structure" could be touched and no light could be turned on without the consent of Walter.

It is easy to see the difficulties these rules imposed upon the investigators. With Dr. Crandon or Dr. Richardson present there was obviously the possibility of a confederate to assist the medium in her performance. With the investigators limited to the dictation of Walter in the use of light and in handling the so-called ectoplasm they were badly hampered. The requirement to dictate everything observed, and to exclude any observations, not so dictated, from a final appraisal of the case was very bad. If an investigator noticed something suspicious and mentioned it to the stenographer, naturally the medium or the confederate would be apprised. Moreover, each investigator knew that if he dictated some of the things he observed the possibilities of his returning for another investigation would be very remote. No one could feel free to dictate exactly as he pleased. Furthermore, it is a serious distraction to dictate when making a close observation. In addition to all that it is not very pleasant to have to put your name to a document, thus endorsing it, which is full of observations made by others. Despite these handicaps the Commission determined to go ahead with the investigation.

In the latter part of January, 1926, while attending

a scientific convention in Boston the three Commissioners had several sittings with Dr. and Mrs. Crandon. After seeing the usual feats the Commission decided that the study of the so-called ectoplasm, or teleplasm would make a good beginning. The following notes are presented to give an idea of the effort to describe what was going on while making observations, and to give an intimate picture of some of the happenings.

January 28, 1926
Sitting at 10 Lime St., Boston, Mass.
Time, 9.08 p.m.

Present: Clockwise, Margery, Dr. Wood, Dr. McComas, Dr. Crandón, Dr. Dunlap, Margery.

Dictating	*Time*	
Dr. McComas		Psyche restless, slight groans, and Dr. Crandon states this is evidence of trance.
Dr. Dunlap		Just before Dr. McComas spoke, Psyche slid Dr. Dunlap's hand from her fingers to her wrist.
Dr. Wood		Psyche's left foot is on my knee.
Dr. Dunlap		Psyche gave me her fingers.
Dr. McComas	9.15	Psyche's head came forward and rests on corner of table near the bell-box.
Dr. McComas	9.26	Both of Psyche's feet are on the floor now.
Dr. McComas	9.31	Psyche straightened out and is resting in her chair with her head apparently on back of chair.

Dr. McComas	9.35	Psyche's left foot is on Dr. Wood's knee and her right foot is on floor near her chair.
Dr. McComas	9.41	Music stopped.
Dr. Dunlap	9.42	Dr. Dunlap is controlling wrist.
Dr. Dunlap	9.43	Dr. Dunlap is now controlling hand.
Dr. Dunlap	9.50	Psyche's right hand is in her lap.
Dr. Dunlap	9.51	Psyche's hand is out again.
Dr. Dunlap	9.54	Both Psyche's ankles are over by Dr. Dunlap, on the floor.
Dr. McComas	9.56	Walter asked for illuminated plaque and Dr. Crandon went to get it.
Dr. McComas	9.58	Dr. Crandon has just returned from the other room with the luminous cardboard plaque, has taken his seat and placed the bell-box on the floor according to instructions from Walter.
Dr. McComas	10.08	Dr. Wood suggested that the plaque was becoming dim so Dr. Crandon took it into the other room to replenish it.
Dr. McComas	10.09	Dr. Crandon has just returned bringing plaque very much brightened. He placed plaque on the table and then placed two handkerchiefs over it.
Dr. McComas	10.14	Walter says he has some teleplasm; it is as far as the edge of the table.
Dr. McComas	10.15	Dr. Dunlap at this point located both of Psyche's feet, with his right hand, under the table.
Dr. Dunlap	10.19	Psyche threw something on the floor with her right hand.
Dr. McComas	10.23	Dr. McComas now sitting apparently opposite Psyche; dark body appears

		on plaque having crossed the first cross line east and west and next to Psyche. Both Psyche's feet are under the table.
Dr. Dunlap	10.30	Teleplasm[1] seems to have disappeared.
Dr. Dunlap	10.36	Teleplasm reappears.
Dr. Dunlap	10.38	Teleplasm again appears, over at third line.
	10.39	Teleplasm gone back.
Dr. Dunlap	10.40	Feet both there.
Dr. Dunlap	10.41	Both feet are down and the teleplasm is still out there.
Dr. Dunlap	10.43	Teleplasm disappeared from my view.
Dr. McComas	10.56	Walter says that he will try and give us visible teleplasm tomorrow night.
	10.59	Sitting ended. Psyche was inspected before and after sitting by stenographer, according to her statement.

Certainly that was not a very interesting session. It was rather tedious waiting an hour for something to happen and when it did to be treated merely with the appearance of a small dark object projecting over a dimly lighted plaque. It will be noted that Dr. Wood sat on one side of Psyche, Mrs. Crandon, and Dr. Dunlap on the other.

The same seating arrangement was used at a later meeting and during the first part of the evening nothing happened. Then I suggested that I take Dr.

---

[1] The word "teleplasm" as used by me means only that the silhouette of *something* appeared.—KNIGHT DUNLAP.

Wood's place beside Psyche and control her left hand and foot. Notice that this does not appear in the notes. We simply forgot to dictate it to the stenographer. When I assumed this position I closed my fingers around Mrs. Crandon's left hand. Nothing happened. Gradually I released my control of her hand and let my hand encircle her wrist. This of course enabled her to use her left hand and I could detect the play of her fingers by the ripple of the muscles in the wrist. And now and then those muscles rippled. After awhile we were rewarded with phenomena. Could I have dictated that into the record? Yes, and my "goodnight" that evening would have been "goodbye" for good.

The following sitting was the most important, most interesting and the last séance that the Commission held.

January 30, 1926
Sitting at 10 Lime St., Boston, Mass.
Time, 9.10 p.m.

Present: Clockwise, Margery, Dr. Wood, Dr. McComas, Dr. Crandon, Dr. Dunlap and back to Margery again.

Dictating	Time	
Dr. Wood	9.10	I am holding Margery's left hand, her left foot is near my right foot and her knees are in contact with my right hand.
Dr. Dunlap	9.10	I am holding Margery's right hand with my hand, knuckle down on her

leg just above the knee, her right foot on my left foot. I have Dr. Crandon's left hand in my right and the combined hands are resting on Dr. Crandon's left knee.

Dr. McComas 9.10 I have Dr. Crandon's right hand and it is resting on his knee, also his head is on my shoulder and he has a capital "C" painted on his sleeve.

There is a luminous spot on Psyche's forehead, a luminous band on each sleeve and a luminous band on each ankle.

The bell-box is on the table in the usual position, that is to say, the platform shelves toward the west (toward Dr. Wood).

Dr. Dunlap 9.15 Dr. Wood rang the bell.

Dr. Wood 9.25 Control very close; no manifestation.

Dr. Wood 9.30 Psyche states that the circle is not properly completed as my hands are touching Dr. Dunlap's. Control changed so as to avoid contact of my hand with that of Dr. Dunlap. No sign of trance.

Dr. Wood 9.40 No sign of trance; no sign of anything. Asked Psyche if she was uncomfortable or wanted the controls changed and she said, "No, she could stand it as long as we could." Psyche laughs at this.

Dr. Dunlap 9.52 Psyche's right hand contracting strongly, gripping my left hand, continuous contractions of the fingers.

Dr. McComas	9.53	My control at present is, my right knee against Psyche's left knee, my left ankle against her right ankle and my fingers around her wrist.
Dr. Wood	9.55	Dr. Wood suggested that the Psyche's knees be in contact with each other and it was done. Dr. Crandon said this would probably prevent the protrusion of the Psyche's telepathic rods which are supposed to issue from the thigh.
Dr. McComas	9.59	The control of the two knees by my right hand has been discontinued.
Dr. Dunlap	10.05	Psyche breathing hard, squeezing my hand.
Dr. McComas	10.07	Psyche's left ankle raised into my lap, my right hand upon Psyche's knee and I am holding her hand.
Dr. McComas	10.17	Walter said, "No she isn't. Hold your horses." My control consists in holding Psyche's left hand and Psyche's feet are in my lap.
Dr. Dunlap	10.17	I am holding Psyche's right hand, resting slightly above her knee and her right foot is now on my left foot.
Dr. McComas	10.20	Walter evidently trying to get force enough to do something. He says, "I never saw such a bunch of stiffs in all my life." He also says, "Talk about dead people; my God!"
Dr. McComas	10.22	Some conversation between Walter and different members of the circle. "Not to be published," says Walter.

Dr. McComas	10.24	Margery's querulous voice said, "I am in awful pain, don't feel good anyhow." Walter replied, "Nobody gives a damn, if you are."
Dr. McComas	10.26	I have both of Psyche's ankles in my lap and her left hand in my right hand.
Dr. Dunlap	10.26	I have Psyche's right hand in my left hand, held upward in the air and it is moving somewhat as she twists.
Dr. McComas	10.30	Something cold and moist slapped me on my hand. Just a moment after, Dr. Dunlap remarked that something cold struck him on the hand. I have both of Psyche's ankles in my lap.
Dr. McComas	10.31	My hand just came in contact with a small ribbed substance which was immediately removed from my hand. I have Psyche's left hand in my right.
Dr. McComas	10.31	Cold, moist substance on my hand again.
Dr. Dunlap	10.31	Psyche's right leg on my lap. Something cold tapped me on the finger.
Dr. McComas	10.32	Cold, ribbed-like substance touched me on thumb and immediately disappeared. Psyche's head constantly moving. Psyche twisting and groaning. Both her ankles are now in my lap.
Dr. McComas	10.35	Psyche constantly repeats, in querulous voice, that she does not feel good.
Dr. McComas	10.36	Luminous doughnut is placed on the table and between myself and

the doughnut appears a dark, rod-like structure, which waves up and down. The rod-like structure has reappeared.

Dr. McComas   10.37   Walter's voice: "Hold your horses, I will show you in a minute."

Dr. McComas   10.38   The rod-like structure moved the doughnut a couple of inches toward Dr. Wood.

Dr. McComas   10.40   Apparently, rod-like structure is lying right across doughnut. Dr. Mc-Comas requested Walter that it bend to right angle. Psyche twisting and writhing as the rod moves.

Dr. Dunlap   10.41   Psyche moved Dr. Dunlap's hand over into contact with a cold, smooth cylindrical something.

Dr. McComas   10.42   Psyche reached over and pressed the back of Dr. McComas' hand on a cold, moist substance.

Dr. McComas   10.45   Dr. McComas' hand directed to the substance which he holds between thumb and forefinger, made some slight impression on same. It seemed like a cylindrical substance about $\frac{3}{4}$ inch in diameter with a hard, bone-like center or axis. Just before this instance, Psyche's voice said, "I feel bad here" and pushed my hand up to the point on this cylindrical substance.

Dr. Dunlap   10.47   The "thing" cold and smooth and soft on my fingers. Psyche's right foot now on mine.

Dr. McComas	10.47	Psyche's left foot on my right foot.
Dr. McComas	10.49	The rod-like structure moved the doughnut.
Dr. Wood	10.50	Something touched my fingers again.
Dr. Dunlap	10.50	The "thing" picked up the doughnut in Wood's hand and moved it around against my head.
Dr. Dunlap	10.51	Psyche presses my hand against "it" again.
Dr. Wood	10.53	My hand was on the table holding the luminous doughnut, teleplasmic rod fell in the palm of my hand, feeling like a rigid rod covered with soft leather. It was placed between my thumb and finger which were holding the doughnut. I squeezed it very hard, which produced no ill effect. The rod then slipped through the doughnut and raised it in the air.
Dr. McComas	10.53	Psyche reached over and pulled my left hand over and placed it upon the teleplasmic structure.
Dr. McComas	10.54	Released control of Psyche's right hand though the bracelet is now visible and has been visible throughout. I now resume control of Psyche's right hand. During the interval in which I did not hold her hand, Dr. Wood did have her hand.
Dr. McComas	10.55	Psyche has taken my right hand and laid it firmly on the "teleplasm." The "teleplasm" is now removed. In this case it was on her hand.

Dr. McComas	11.00	Both of Psyche's ankles are in my lap. While speaking, felt a touch of "teleplasm" on my little finger. The "teleplasm" apparently against Psyche's right leg, above the knee.
Dr. Dunlap	11.02	Back of my hand touched by "it" again. It is now touching my fingers.
Dr. Dunlap	11.04	My hand was put over and between my fingers I felt of "it." It is cold, soft, with rigid ruler-like core. I cannot say whether it is a single or multiple core.
Dr. McComas	11.05	Received rather sharp touch on left hand which is resting on the table, I should judge, about a foot from her body, just the other side of Psyche's two ankles.
Dr. Dunlap	11.07	The teleplasmic rod picked doughnut out of my hand, held it several inches above the table, moving it around. In levitation now.
Dr. Wood	11.07	Holding both Dr. Crandon's hands during this levitation.
Dr. McComas	11.09	Doughnut waving up and down, sideways; now seems to be nearer to me. Doughnut now resting on table. Psyche has taken right leg from my lap and put it on Dr. Dunlap's foot.
Dr. Wood	11.10	Doughnut starting to rise from table with upward movement parallel with movement of luminous band on Psyche's head.

Dr. Wood	11.12	Doughnut is now moving again without any movement of Psyche's head.
Dr. Dunlap	11.12	While levitating, teleplasmic rod struck my fingers. A moment ago, rod touched my fingers again.
Dr. McComas	11.14	Doughnut has dropped to the floor. Several minutes levitation of doughnut.
Dr. McComas	11.15	At my request my hand was taken and placed upon teleplasmic rod. The teleplasmic rod was standing up in the air. My hand closed around it. Apparently it is very firm with a slightly ruffled effect.
Dr. Dunlap	11.16	I have the rod in my hand. Psyche put my hand over and put the rod between my fingers, pushing my hand along so that the rod pushed through my fingers several inches. It was cold.
Dr. McComas	11.17	Teleplasmic rod touched my cheek.
Dr. Dunlap	11.18	On cheek, scratching my ear (McComas touching my hand), rapping me on the top of the head and on the back of the head. (Joke)
Dr. Dunlap	11.19	Walter rapped on the table with the teleplasmic rod, stating he was rapping on my head but he did not.
Dr. Wood	11.20	During the rapping episode, I was holding Dr. Crandon's head in my left hand and Dr. Crandon's face was in contact with my hand.
Dr. Dunlap	11.21	During the rapping phenomena and when I was touched with the rod

		on the head, I was holding Psyche's right hand and Dr. Crandon's left hand.
Dr. McComas	11.21	During the time that the teleplasmic rod was striking at Dr. Dunlap's head, Psyche's ankles were in my lap. One of them passed out at one time but came immediately back, then both of them were out and came back immediately. Psyche's body was twisting and turning constantly. Psyche turned around in her chair and was apparently over on her right thigh at the time of the strokes upon Dr. Dunlap's head.
Dr. McComas	11.23	Dr. McComas feeling Psyche from thigh to knee finds tights. This search made at Dr. Crandon's suggestion.
Dr. Dunlap	11.23	Dr. Dunlap finds that Psyche has silk bloomers (tights) on.
Dr. McComas	11.25	Several times Psyche's left hand slipped through mine so that I had her wrist for a moment, but I have always been in contact with her hand or her wrist.
Dr. Dunlap	11.25	I have had Psyche's right hand all the time as I recollect.
Dr. McComas	11.26	Psyche said, "I have cramps here" and taking Dr. McComas hand placed it on her abdomen at about the umbilical region. Dr. McComas can feel a belt. (Dr. Crandon adds that the Psychic is at present unwell.)

Dr. McComas	11.30	Psyche has one foot in my lap and one foot on the table and I have her left hand.
Dr. McComas	11.31	Psyche's right leg went to the floor and came back again. Walter's voice informs me that I am a liar.
Dr. McComas	11.32	Psyche's two feet are down now resting on my foot and on Dr. Dunlap's foot.
Dr. McComas	11.32	Just before Psyche came out of the trance, she drew my hand over, placed it on her stomach just below the umbilical region and it remained there for possibly ten seconds.
Dr. Dunlap	11.33	We have broken our control.

The stenographer (Miss Barbaro) reported that she examined and found the psychic unwell before the sitting and found her still unwell after the sitting.

There was nausea and vomiting of the psychic after the sitting.

Sitting closed at 11.33 p.m.

Several interesting incidents occurred which do not appear in the notes. After the sitting was over Mrs. Crandon was sitting in the open cabinet and the lights were turned on. Some one suggested that the record should be made trustworthy by having a thorough examination of Mrs. Crandon and the cabinet at once. Here occurred the cleverest repartee any medium ever made. Mrs. Crandon coughed, gagged, leaned over as though suffering from violent *mal de mer*. Then aided by the stenographer she hurried to the bathroom and we could hear a very good imitation of a passenger crossing the English Channel. Dr. Crandon left the room to see his wife. We took a flashlight and examined the floor as we felt that Psyche had been firing blank cartridges. She had.

Since we had been told that we had the freedom of the house Dr. Dunlap and I returned to 10 Lime Street the next day. Being told that the Crandons were out we proceeded to the séance room to look things over carefully. We had not been there long before Mrs. Crandon entered and our Sherlock Holmes work abruptly ceased. Mrs. Crandon seemed to be in the pink of health, laughing and talking in good spirits.

I mention this because Dr. Crandon insisted that Dr. Wood's rough handling of the teleplasm made Margery sick for a number of days and caused considerable loss of weight. Indeed this incident was used by Dr. Crandon to terminate any further investigation by this Commission. Perhaps he also heard Dr. Wood say to me after Mrs. Crandon's hasty retreat, "Shall I expose her now?" Possibly he also heard me say, "No, this is not the time." At all events Dr. Crandon found reasons to rule out both of my fellow Commissioners, though he retained a friendly feeling toward me.

Later as the Special Research Officer of the American Society for Psychical Research I tried to make up another Commission but I could never succeed in satisfying Dr. Crandon. I believe Mrs. Crandon had the courage and the ingenuity to face another Commission. My reason for this comes from one of the most amusing incidents that occurred at Number 10 Lime Street. I had been urging the doctor to have another scientific study of the case. Suddenly Margery said, "Let's go ask Walter." Up into the familiar dark room we went. Margery sat in her open cabinet, the doctor beside her. Quickly Walter jumped into the discussion. He was all for any kind of an investigation anybody wanted. Dr. Crandon objected to everything, but Margery's brother beat him at every point. While I listened to the dialogue occasionally putting in a little argument for my next Commission, I could not help thinking that here was a unique way for a wife to manage her husband. It was simple and effective. So I thought at the time. However, I never got my Commission and after months of fruitless effort I finally sent the following report signed by the entire Commission to the Society:

April 18, 1927.
4100 North Charles St.,
Baltimore, Md.

The Research Committee,
American Society for Psychical Research,
15 Lexington Ave.,
New York City, N. Y.

Gentlemen:
    The undersigned submit this report to you at this time for the following reasons: Dr. Crandon is taking advantage of

the delay in the appearance of a report to spread the impression that the Commission as a whole has not found unfavorably for the Margery mediumship, and also it has now become evident that Dr. Crandon will not permit any member of the Commission to carry on an investigation of a genuinely scientific character.

Your Commissioners had several sittings with Dr. and Mrs. Crandon in the last week of January, 1926, which were reported stenographically at the time of the sittings. These reports were sent you immediately after the sittings and it is unnecessary at this time, therefore, to discuss the sittings in detail. The purpose of the present report is to give you the conclusions of your Commissioners based on the observations of these sittings, the reports of others, and some experiments of our own.

The sittings which were allotted to your Commissioners were for observational purposes only, and no controls devised by us were imposed upon Mrs. Crandon and no experiments were planned and consummated in the seance room. It was our intention to observe the effects Dr. and Mrs. Crandon produced and to make our experiments later.

At the first sitting there were many of the friends of the Crandons present to whom we were introduced. Some of them constituted what Dr. Crandon termed his Advanced Circle. It was intended by the Crandons to be an evening in which the usual effects should be presented for our observation. There was one effect, however, which they told us was a novelty. This consisted in rendering luminous paint, which had lost its fluorescence in the dark, luminescent. A disc with a hollow centre had been painted with luminous paint and had become dark. We were told that "Walter's" terminal would cause the "doughnut" to glow. When the doughnut became luminescent the friends of the Crandons exclaimed with pleasure and congratulated "Walter" upon his achievement.

Dr. Wood reproduced this effect in his laboratory at the

Johns Hopkins University, using a pocket flashlight and an
ultra-violet filter. This phenomenon is a baffling one to people
who are unacquainted with the action of luminous paint in the
presence of very short light waves. Dr. Crandon had ample
opportunity to employ a pocket flash light in this way, and
actually had a flashlight in his pocket on the side towards the
medium at the sitting.

The bell-box was featured in these sittings as an especially
remarkable phenomenon. Dr. Dunlap noted the change in the
tension of the steel spring during a sitting. He constructed a
box in which the spring was enclosed in the body of the box, and
could be adjusted for various tensions. This arrangement pre-
cluded any tampering with the spring. Dr. Dunlap was never
permitted to substitute his box for the one the Crandons had
been using. In two boxes made after the pattern of the
Crandon box the same effects that the Crandons obtained were
obtained by taking the tension from the spring during the
sitting and they prevented short-circuiting the connecting
wires, which are outside the box in the Crandon arrangement,
and which can readily be short-circuited by using a needle,
thus causing the bell to ring.

Your Commissioners were informed by Dr. Crandon that
psychic rods protruded from the body of the medium. He
stated that they were very sensitive and could perceive the
pips on playing cards and could identify various small objects
and wooden letters in complete darkness. At the last sitting
one member of the Commission squeezed the end of such an
alleged rod and neither Margery nor "Walter" were aware of the
fact until it was dictated for the stenographer.

Dr. Crandon had stated that the extreme sensitivity of
these "psychic rods" showed how intimately they were connected with the vitality of the medium. He argued that any
vigorous handling of such rods might injure the medium.
After the incident above described the sitting continued for

forty minutes with the rod in vigorous activity. After the sitting one of your Commissioners suggested that Mrs. Crandon remain in the cabinet until the light was turned on and that a search then be made. When Mrs. Crandon heard this she began to gag and cough as though ill. She bent forward as though vomiting and hurried from the room. An examination showed nothing upon the floor and the stomachic performance seemed simulated.

In the opinion of Dr. Dunlap the "psychic rod" employed on this occasion, as judged by feeling and by usual observation in the dim light, was the intestine of some animal, showing the stumps of some blood vessels and stuffed with some substance like cotton, through which ran several wires.

The next day Dr. Dunlap and Dr. McComas visited the Crandon house and did not find Mrs. Crandon any the worse for her experience; she ran up and down the stairs easily and seemed in excellent spirits. These details are mentioned because Dr. Crandon has maintained that his wife was made ill from the squeezing of the so-called "teleplastic rod."

From the time of this incident it was impossible to have further sittings as a Commission. We had provided in our Convention to have any disagreements adjusted by a committee of three. Dr. Crandon would not have recourse to this agreement. He continually refused to have further sittings but would not give his reasons to the Commission.

In the summer of 1926 your Society engaged Dr. McComas as a Special Research Officer. He attended a number of sittings with Mrs. Crandon but was not permitted to try any tests with the medium. He succeeded on one occasion in greatly improving the controls for Mrs. Crandon but was not permitted to continue and to impose controls upon Dr. Crandon and his associates. After several months of effort to experiment he abandoned that method of investigation as impossible while Dr. Crandon had control of the situation. He then

sought to duplicate the "Margery phenomena." Professor
Grant H. Code, of the University of Delaware, reproduced the
levitation effects excellently; he also reproduced the bell-box
effect and the reading of the cards in the dark.

Dr. McComas held two séances in his office at the Society's
building, using a Hindoo for the "medium." These meetings
were attended by members of the Society who had had wide
experience in psychic research. Some fifteen of these sitters
voluntarily signed statements to the effect that these phenomena were done by no normal means known to them. Five
of the sitters had seen the Margery phenomena and agreed that
these were quite as good as Margery's. These phenomena consisted in the ringing of the bell-box, whistling and whispering
by the medium using a voice cut-out of the Richardson type,
reading cards in the dark and the appearance of psychic lights.

These effects and those obtained by Professor Code are
excellent duplicates of the Crandon performances.

In view of the above findings your Commission submits
that the Margery mediumship is a clever and entertaining performance but is unworthy of any serious consideration by your
Society.

We submit further that the unwillingness of Dr. Crandon
to allow the Commission to proceed with the investigation is
a sufficient indication that no investigation by competent
investigators employing the methods and checks required in
all scientific research is likely to be permitted.

For some reason the American Society for Psychical Research did not feel inclined to publish this report. It was treated the way Dr. Rhine's report
was treated when he submitted his findings that
indicated the Crandons were playing tricks.

And now we must admit that all the scientific attempts to study Margery came to no conclusions as

to just how her feats were performed. The reason
was, of course, that the investigations were stopped
whenever they found a good lead. In my own case
I had urged that a stethoscope be placed on the medium's throat which would have told instantly
whether a whisper came from that source. Of course
this was denied me. Then I urged that I might run
Margery and Walter through an association test.
This would very clearly have proved any identity of
the two. That was denied me, as the doctor said
it savored of psycho-analysis. Then I wanted to
cross examine Walter about some of his doings in
this vale of tears. I had learned from an intimate
friend a great deal about the young man, and some
shocking episodes that he could not forget if he had
lived to be a hundred. I never had a chance.

With some amusement and sympathy I watched
the development of this famous Boston case. It appeared that the thumb-print of Walter had been
found on an old razor blade. It was a curious print
with a strongly marked scar in it. There would not
be one chance in many millions of another thumb
carrying those lines and that scar. Imagine the
amazement and delight of Margery's admirers when
Walter decided to materialize his thumb and give
them fresh duplicates of the old print. Duplicates
in plenty he gave them. And now the terrible anti-
climax. The faithful and long suffering Mr. E. E.
Dudley discovered that it was the thumb-print of a
Boston dentist!

CHAPTER IX

MY OWN SÉANCE

FOR nearly a year I had been trying to come to grips with Dr. Crandon. Never could I quite reach him. Always I was held off. It made me feel the way I used to when I was a small boy and wanted to wrestle with a tall boy. Every time I would reach his shoulder, or swing my arms hoping to catch his knees, that long arm would hold me off so that I could never accomplish a grip. So there seemed to me only one thing to do and that was to reproduce the Margery phenomena. If this were done it would at least be one answer to the Society's inquiry, "Is Margery genuine?" Though it would not explain how Margery did her feats, it would at least be a challenge to Lime Street and would argue that the good doctor should be more amenable to real tests. Indeed, I invited the doctor to come to my séance some time and see if he could explain my "phenomena."

Little did I imagine what I was getting into when I planned a séance of my own. Positively it is one of the most exciting experiences any one can have. I have fished in many waters and have shot different sorts of game but I have never known a thrill to match that of saving your medium from an exposure

147

just in the nick of time.   Indeed, there is not a dull
moment during the whole evening when you are con-
ducting a séance.   Effects must be had and you must
lead up to them.   Constantly on the defensive you
cannot let anything suspicious bob up during the
evening.   Dull moments there may be for the sitters
but there is never a dull moment for the medium or
the master of ceremonies.

To duplicate Dr. Crandon's séance it was necessary
to get "atmosphere," not a little but a lot, for I was
extending invitations to connoisseurs.   More than
that, I was going to have some sitters who had been
to see Margery and it was necessary to give as convincing an exhibition as she did.   Consequently, I
was puzzled about my atmosphere.   I found it, however, in a most unexpected way.

In New York there is a very wise, little man who
sells apparatus for magicians.   He does not show you
all his wares the first few times you visit his unpre-
tentious shop.   After you have proven that you are
one of the elect you may get into his back room.   As
I was much interested in building an apparition and
had already done some experimenting with luminous
paint, anthracine and the ultra-violet ray, I gained
access to the sanctum.   There, as I explained what
sort of cloth I needed and how the paint was to be
applied, I excited the curiosity of another customer,
a Hindoo.   He, too, was in the apparition business.
We compared notes.   He claimed his apparition was

the best that had been produced. To prove it he cited a séance he had held for a half a dozen physicians, a short time before. According to his account every one of his sitters were convinced that they had seen something supernatural. No wonder! This is what he did. Seated in a large arm chair he dropped into a deep trance. Then on the wall behind him, in the darkened room, a face glowed suddenly in clear vision of all the men. Turning on the light and rushing to the wall they could find nothing to account for the strange appearance. Then I knew I had found my atmosphere,—this Hindoo.

The next important accomplishment was to duplicate Dr. Crandon's clever arrangement for preventing sitters' changing their minds. During a sitting and immediately afterwards a sitter is often puzzled. Maybe for the moment he is quite convinced that he has witnessed something supernormal. That is the time to get him to commit himself. Then he cannot say, the next morning, that he knew it was a farce all along. To accomplish this I had my sitters sign the following memorandum if they cared to do so. "On the evening of January the twenty-seventh, Ran Chandra had a sitting at the American Society for Psychical Research, in which four of the phenomena of the Margery mediumship were reproduced. Cards were identified in the dark. A bell-box was rung, as Margery rings hers. A voice cut-out was used, similar to that of Dr. Richardson's, and psychic

lights were obtained. The observers signed a statement to the effect that: 'These phenomena were
observed by me and I further state that they were
done by no normal means known to me.' " Fifteen
of the sitters signed this memorandum and several
of these had seen the Margery séances.

Of course it was not practicable to reproduce all
the things that Margery had done. That would have
taken too long and would have required considerable
rehearsing. So I selected some of the things which
were most frequently done in the famous little room
at Number Ten Lime Street.

After a little rehearsing I felt that my Hindoo was
prepared to do his part. I did not give him any opportunities to vary the program. Indeed I needed
him only for atmosphere. Any one could have fitted
into his rôle with a little training. But as a producer
of atmosphere he was magnificent. I introduced
him, after allowing the sitters to examine the room,
and called attention to the fact that the Hindoos had
been interested in occultism long before our civilization was started. What Margery did, I maintained,
were but kindergarten performances for the Hindoo.
Then to give the situation a Crandon touch I urged
them to be their own observers and draw their own
conclusions. I went further. I stated that I was in
no position to endorse the genuineness of what he did
and that I had always believed that all such phenomena should be carefully observed before coming

to any conclusions.   This may seem as though a cool
blanket was thrown over the proceedings at the out-
set.   If that were the case what followed quickly
counteracted such an effect.   The Hindoo rose, an
impressive figure.   From head to foot streamed a
long white robe, and above his cleancut, Oriental face
was a resplendent gold turban.   In a voice that no
one could resist he urged them to bear with him as
he led in a prayer to his own Invisible Spirit in the
ancient Sanskrit language.   Even I felt moved.
And I knew that his only acquaintance with Sanskrit
was the alphabet which he had been repeating.

In front of the Hindoo was a little wooden table
around which we were all seated.   My place was next
to the Hindoo, just as Dr. Crandon usually sat next
to Margery.   The sitters were given a pack of cards
in the dark from which they could select any card
they wished.   It was so very dark that no one could
see the pips on the face of the cards.   After they had
slipped one out of the pack they would place it on
the table, and in a few moments the Hindoo would
tell them what was the number and the suit of the
card.   Then each sitter would retake his card and,
remembering how it had been named, would wait
until the light was turned on to verify it.   In only a
few cases were there any errors.   Usually these occurred with face cards.   Indeed, it was a very convincing performance; the room was so dark and the
replies were so prompt that it seemed impossible for

anyone to read the cards. The explanation current around the table was that it must be done by means of ectoplasm or teleplasm, which could feel the pips on the cards.

Behind the scenes this is what went on. Just behind my chair lay my hat and coat. I reached back, caught up the hat and handed it to the Hindoo. Inside the hat was a little luminous paint. All that this modern exponent of the ancient mysteries had to do was to hold the hat before him, reach out and pick up a card, hold it near the luminous paint, read it and slip it back on the table. Simple? Not so very. Let that luminous paint stand for twenty minutes and it does not throw enough glow to read anything. So that experiment has to be done shortly after the séance starts or you are lost. On the other hand if you get too much luminous paint it will reflect on the white robe and then there is nothing to do but go home.

The next entry was my *chef d'oeuvre*. On the table rested a simple bell-box, built on the Crandon pattern. It was a small box which contained two dry-cell batteries and a little bell. Exactly the sort of thing that everyone has in his house to ring the door bell. Instead of a push button to ring the bell I had a broad, wooden flap on top of the box lid. When it was pressed down from an angle of about forty-five degrees, at which it was held by a spring, it would bring two pieces of copper together and ring the bell.

All of the wiring could be traced very easily and anyone could see the whole apparatus in all of its sim-
plicity. Everyone was invited to inspect the box and
to satisfy himself that there were no trick gadgets in
it. Then when the light was turned out and all had
joined hands around the table so that no one could
reach out and press the flap to ring the bell the spirit
of the Hindoo would be called upon to press down
that flap and ring the bell as a sitter might wish.
This worked very nicely. A sitter would call for
two short rings and a long one or three long rings and
the box responded according to the request. This
was very impressive as all hands were joined and no
foot could reach the box.

Even more striking was the performance of the
box when a faint light was allowed in the room.
Then it behaved as did Crandon's box. A sitter was
allowed to pick it up, hold it in his hands, swing it
around in a circle and satisfy himself that there were
no threads or wires controlling it. The box began to
ring the moment it was taken from the table and kept
on ringing continuously or intermittently while it was
being held. It ceased the moment it was placed back
upon the table. Each sitter was told that this was
what would happen and when it did happen it made a
strong impression. Then in a good strong light the
box was examined and no evidence of trickery could
be found. Indeed, I shall never forget the expression
on the face of an elderly professional man who care-

fully raised the box and discovered that it rang according to specifications and also that it stopped as had been predicted. I was anxious to see if he would sign the memorandum. He did. That box was convincing.

Again let us go behind the scenes. The medium had nothing to do with the ringing of the box. While we tried to work up "power" by singing "The Battle Hymn of the Republic" I slipped out of my seat and caught a thread around the spring that held up the flap. The other end I held in my mouth. That enabled anyone to hold my hands and those of the medium and did not interfere with the flapping of the flap. All I had to do was to throw my head back to produce a signal. Then when that part of the performance was over I would start chewing on the thread until I had pulled it off the spring and worked its entire length into my mouth.

Ringing the bell by lifting the box from the table was not so simple a procedure. That box *was* tricky. It had a very heavy bottom which was not fastened very tightly. When it was lifted the bottom would sag down a fraction of an inch. As the wires were attached to this bottom and ran from there to the flap, when the bottom went down the flap went too and the little bell rang. To prevent this from happening when people were inspecting the box I would straighten the spring and lift the flap so high that the slight pull of the bottom could not bring the cop-

per contacts together. After the signals had been
given it was my nice job to slip out of the chair as
the "Battle Hymn of the Republic" was being sung
again and press the spring down to a place where
the pull of the bottom would bring the contacts together. That is where I got some thrills. This sort
of thing has to be done while there is some noise
going on. Consequently there must be a pause in the
proceedings as though the power had disappeared.
To get it back there must be some loud singing and
under the cover of that one can make some unob-
served noises of his own. On one occasion I was
groping around the box and my fingers interlaced
with a hand coming from the other side of the table.
Now there is only one thing to do in such a predicament and that is nothing. Fortunately the sitter
who was doing this investigating said nothing. After
the séance was over I engaged him in conversation.
I told him that I was doing a little investigating and
had reached out to explore the box. I asked him if
it was his hand with which I had come in contact.
Imagine my surprise when he exclaimed:

"Good heavens! Was that your hand? I thought
it was a piece of ectoplasm."

That young man was a graduate from a famous
university!

I should have mentioned that we had constructed
a sort of cabinet within which the medium could sit.
It was merely some timbers nailed together with

some cloths thrown over them and so arranged that the medium's hands could be lashed tightly to the sides of the cabinet. Of course we had quite a little ceremony in trussing up the Hindoo hand and foot. The fastenings had to be examined so that everyone was satisfied that he could not get a hand or foot free. Then it was explained to the group that the Hindoo had a spirit which controlled him. As Margery had her "Walter" so Ran Chandra had his "Gogol." With Margery, Walter chatted alongside her head. The Hindoo was more canny; he left you to guess where his Gogol was. Of course it was necessary to use a whisper, for they are hard to identify. The voice of a little girl and that of an old man are easily distinguished; but each, with a little practice, can develop whispers that no one can distinguish. Gogol whispered. You could hear him deep in the cabinet and all you needed to complete the mystery was the recollection of the "voice cut-out."

This voice cut-out was my own invention. It was built on the same pattern as that of Dr. Richardson. A large U-tube stood in a rack on the table in front of the cabinet. From one arm of the tube a heavy rubber tubing ran to the medium's mouth. Instead of Dr. Richardson's nipple I used a simple glass funnel. When this was slipped into the mouth and held between the gums and the lips, with the tongue inserted in the funnel's opening not a word could be articulated. To prove that the tongue was inserted in the funnel it was necessary to blow in the tube, thus changing the level of the water in the U-tube. As long as the tongue was inserted the water could be held at a low level in one arm of the U-tube and at a high level in the other. While this was done no one's mouth could be used for any other purpose. Eash sitter was allowed to satisfy himself that this was true.

After the Hindoo had been properly secured in the cabinet so that he could not use his hands or feet, the funnel was inserted into his mouth. Then the lights were turned out. Everyone waited with breathless expectancy. Nothing happened. To help the flagging power "The Battle Hymn of the Republic" was sung once more. After its stirring strains had faded a whisper could be heard coming from the cabinet. Light though it was it carried some heavy philosophy. It did not stoop to trivial things. It did not bring sketchy and ambiguous messages from the dead. Rather it reflected the deep learning of ancient India. It was impressive.

It seemed to me that this feat was more convincing to the sitters than anything else we did. I felt that it was mystifying and convincing because I had puzzled for some weeks over this very performance with Margery. There really was no way the Hindoo could get his hands free to get the tube out of his mouth. No confederate was needed for this performance and I could remain in my chair. The sitters could hear me speaking from where I sat.   Indeed, I believe a good magician would be badly puzzled to explain this phenomenon.

Behind the scenes this is what went on.   In that long, heavy rubber tube were two little valve seats and a small steel ball rolled between them.   When the breath was blown into the tube and the tube was either raised or lowered the little ball would roll into one or the other of the valve seats.   Once firmly lodged in a seat it would stop the movement of air. All that was necessary to hold the water at any level desired was to blow in the tube, lower it and allow the little ball to close the valve.   Then the mouth could be freed from the funnel and messages given at will.   To hold the tube snugly without the use of the hand, it was only necessary to grasp it between the knees.   It was sufficiently rigid to remain in an upright position while the funnel was slipped from the mouth.

One night something went wrong with one of the valves.   Wait as we would and sing as we did, Gogol would not whisper.   Everyone became impatient. I knew that something had gone wrong but I could not imagine what.   In such a predicament there is only one thing to do; get more power.   So they sang and I investigated.   That valve would not work. I had to crouch down beside the cabinet, take the funnel out of the medium's mouth, blow the water up so that everyone could see the two corks lit up

with luminous paint change their positions. There
I remained until the Gogol had told about this life
and the life to come. It seemed an eternity to me.
What could I do if someone addressed a remark to
"the doctor?" Nor was that the worst of it. I had
to find my way back to the chair in the dark after
the messages had ceased.

There was one thing that I was very anxious to
achieve at these sittings. I wanted to go Margery
one better and have a good apparition appear in view
of everyone. On one side of the room I had hung a
large sheet. Upon this the wise, little man who sold
magician apparatus had painted a human face in
anthracine. To make this glow in the dark it is
necessary to throw an ultra-violet ray upon it. These
rays cannot be seen as they stream across a dark
room. In my pocket I had a strong flashlight with
an ultra-violet filter. My puzzle was to get the filter
adjusted to the flash and then make the beams hit
the right place on the sheet. In the rehearsal everything went nicely. From the sheet a face glowed
clearly the moment the rays struck the paint. With
a little practice I could make the face flash out and
disappear so quickly that it was impossible to do
more than get the impression of a human face. Exposures of about one second gave the best effect.
Longer exposures betrayed the fact that the face was
painted.

Good magicians and mediums do not take long

chances. That rules me out of their class. I took a chance by putting a fresh battery in my flashlight at the first sitting. It made the light so strong that I had to give up my effort. Try as I would I could not adjust that light. On the second occasion I did succeed in having the face show on the wall for an instant. Unfortunately only a few of the sitters observed it. To them it was very impressive. Curious things can happen in a séance. Once I left the filter off by mistake and snapped my flashlight in the direction of the sheet. For an instant the sheet flashed white. All that side of the room was illuminated. I was sure that I had ruined everything and that my séance was completely spoiled. Surprisingly enough, few people noticed it. Those that did were delighted. Never had they seen such a spread of psychic light before.

Surely luck was with me that evening, some good and some bad. Bad luck followed that flashlight and the filter. At a critical moment, as I tried to slip the filter over the flashlight it slipped from my fingers and fell to the floor. I could not find it anywhere and I did not dare to explore too far. It would have been bad technique to bump my head against some sitter's knees. While I was gingerly groping about on the floor losing my good disposition at a rapid rate one of the lady sitters who prided herself on her acumen remarked:

"Dr. McComas, did you hear something rap?"

Dr. McComas had to seat himself on a chair to make his voice come from a natural position and then assume a casual tone,—"Why, what did it sound like?"

"It sounded like a spirit rap but too metallic. I never heard a spirit rap sound metallic. Do you suppose it was a spirit rap?"

I was not in a position to defend a spirit rap at that moment, so I took my watch chain and hit it on the side of the table and asked her if that was the sound she heard, telling her that it was my watch chain against the table.

"Oh, that was it," she exclaimed, relieved, "I could not imagine how a spirit rap could have sounded so metallic. All that I have heard had dull sound."

Now was that good luck.

You may infer from this last episode that I had some very good sitters in my circle, and indeed I did. They not only helped my own performances along, but two of them staged a performance of their own. Out of the floor in the midst of the circle two ladies saw a luminous form arise. Each assisted the other in describing it, the faintness of the light, its curious movements, its growing dimensions. Since this was my first experience in managing a séance I became fidgety. What was going to happen? If they got hysterical it would put my whole evening in bad repute. If they constructed a beautiful apparition which no one else could see the other sitters would

attribute it to imagination. It did not seem that I
could afford to have anything happen which would
cheapen the séance. So I decided to divert their attention. Now it never would do to deliberately call
two seers away from their vision. That would lay
one open to all sorts of criticism. It occurred to me
that if they put their minds on anything else the
apparition would evaporate Therefore I suggested
that we try to get a little more power in order to see
what might develop and asked that we sing "The
Battle Hymn of the Republic." To a man who comes
from the South that tune is not an especial favorite.
When he has heard it a thousand times in a dark room
it is apt to jangle his nerves. On this occasion I
enjoyed it, for it chased away the apparition and
saved my séance.

In numerous séances sitters speak of feeling psychic
breezes. Cool air blows against the cheeks, hands
or ankles. At my séance I had made no arrangements to produce these effects. Nevertheless a number of people declared that they felt them. This is
a good illustration of what can happen when you have
the right atmosphere at a sitting.

Throughout the whole of the evening I had been
dreading the moment when the lights should go on
and I should ask my sitters if they would sign the
memorandum. That would tell the story of the success of the meeting. Though everything had gone
along very smoothly and there had been no hostility,

I could not tell what critical attitude might be building up in the minds of some of those present. After a séance is over and people begin to compare notes the very good impression that the séance gave as a whole can readily be dispelled by the remarks of someone who knows just how to explain everything. Happily no such condition arose. Over half of my sitters willingly signed the paper. The others were not critical or hostile but simply did not wish to commit themselves.

Shortly after the séance I wrote to the people who had participated and told them that the Hindoo and I had worked up these effects in order to show Dr. Crandon that what Margery did could be done by natural means and that Dr. Crandon should permit an investigation much more thorough-going than any that he had allowed up to date. Some of my sitters took it all in good part, others were somewhat indignant.

CHAPTER X

REPORTED AND REPUTED

ONE of the things that first impressed me in reading the proceedings of The British Society for Psychical Research was the apparent correctness of a number of messages given by mediums. As the person who received the message commented upon what "came through" it was indeed surprising to find so many things that were pertinent to the investigator's life. In fact, it remained a mystery to me until I, myself, began to report upon what a medium gave me and then the experience showed up the subject in an entirely new light.

As you read the first account of my sitting with Mrs. Sanders I think you will notice its similarity to many of the accounts that appear in the magazines published by Psychic Research Societies. Indeed, when I returned to the Society and read my notes with their comments to the young lady then acting as secretary she exclaimed that it was the most "veridical and evidential" material that she had seen during her connection with the Society.

Sitting with Mrs. Sanders, July 27, 1926.

Medium: I get the initial J. Also an L, a woman's name. She passed out three months ago.

(*Note:* The pronouncing of the J and L suggested to me the name of a friend, Gillet, who had died about nine months previously. However the medium did not get the final syllable of the name. My friend, however, was a man.)

Medium: The spirit of a gentleman is here. I see an old house among the trees, part of it is falling down. The word Illinois comes to me.

(*Note:* The word Illinois has no significance that I can discover. I always associate an old colonial house with my friend G, for there we spent some of the happiest days of my life.)

Medium: Also an H. A spirit of a lady, motherly, not dead long. Abdominal trouble. She comes close to me. Her name begins with Em or M. Is perhaps forty or forty-five. Has dark hair, parted in the middle. Had three daughters. One daughter's name begins with an M, the other with a P. She asks how A or J are.

(*Note:* The H is the initial of my first name. The motherly lady fits very closely my maternal grandmother. She was very much older than forty-five at the time of her death, but was very young in appearance. She wore a wig, with rather dark hair, which was parted in the middle. Her name was Mary. She had two daughters, one named Mary and the other Phoebe. My grandmother was very fond of two men who married two of her grand-daughters, a Jim and an Albert.)

M: Two parts of the family lived together while this lady was living.

(*Note:* My father and mother lived with my grandmother and her daughter in my grandmother's country home during the summer months.)

M: Is there a Jim?

Sitter: Yes, there is a Jim.

M: How is Jim? Sends her love to him. There has been some trouble three months ago. Something was sold. Did C have anything to do with it? I seem to get a C. Is it a C?

Sitter: No, it is an O.

M: Yes, that is right. It is an O.

(*Note:* The Jim mentioned is the husband of her grand-daughter, of whom she was very fond. When mention was made of something sold three months before I at once thought of my brother who had sold it and suggested an O for a C as the two letters are much alike in appearance.)

M: A man passed out near the old house. The name was W. He was probably shot. I get a Robert, Robert B. Or is it Robert C? Watkins, Wadley? No, it doesn't come quite clear. He calls you Henry.

(*Note:* The following incident was suggested to me by the reference to the old house: a Robinson C. Waters was nearly shot by me in a boyish escapade near this old house. Of course he is not the one who passed out, but while I was there an elderly man was nearing death and died some time after I left. "He calls you Henry"; this is the first time that the medium mentioned my name, and she did so without the least hesitation, as coming from the lips of a friend who had known me since I was eleven years old.)

M: Are there five in the family?

Sitter: No, four.

M: Are you the last?

Sitter: No, third.

M: Don't they call you Doctor?

Sitter: Yes.

(*Note:* Though this came with no hesitation, it cannot be taken as evidential, for I was referred to in a phone conversation as "Doctor.")

M: There seems to be a woman who might also be called Doctor. She is with you. She is very close to you. Don't know whether you are an M.D. or a D.D. Would her name be M? Also her name sounds like Laura.

(*Note:* I have a cousin, a trained nurse, whose name is "Em."

She lived for many years with her mother, Laura. We were closely associated in the upbringing of another cousin. There was a member of this family, a sister to Laura, who was often called "Doc," playfully, and who passed on six months before.)

M: I find you three months ago having trouble. Something has to be cancelled. She calls "Hebe." She has crimpy hair, gray-blue eyes. Has very little hair.

(*Note:* The reference to the trouble three months ago has been explained. The cancelling probably had to do with a certain phase of the negotiations. "She calls 'Hebe.'" The medium did not get this very clear. If it were the grandmother, the name could well have been Phoebe. "She has crimpy hair, very little hair." This description of the hair is quite apropos as the lady in question had very scanty hair and wore a wig with a crimpy, wavy effect in it. The gray blue eyes also fit the picture nicely.)

M: I am speaking of a young woman who is with her. She died of a fever, due to an accident. Her name is S or B. Weren't you near death in October or August?

Sitter: Yes, in October some years ago.

(*Note:* The young woman referred to may well be the granddaughter of the older woman with the crimpy hair. Her name did begin with B. I am not informed concerning her death. I think there was an anaemia. I know of no accident that preceded her death. My information, however, is lacking in these details. Several years ago I nearly died from appendicitis, the attack occurring late in October.)

M: You have a brother who is a doctor. No? Oh, it's a close friend. His name begins with a T or an F. He has a relation in the spirit land.

(*Note:* My brother was not a doctor, but many of my friends in the academic world are called by the title "doctor." Of these there are not a few whose name begins with a T or an F. I do not think, however, of any close friend with these initials.)

M: Bob says tell you Jeff is with him.

Sitter laughs.

M: Do you recognize Jeff?

Sitter: I wonder.   Isn't he a colored man?

M: Yes, that is it.   He is a colored man.

Sitter: Did he die of drink?

M: Yes, that is Jeff.

(*Note:* At once when the names Bob and Jeff were mentioned my thoughts went back to some amusing incidents involving the old house in the country, the Robert that I associated with it and a darkey who was always drinking "giant tonic."   I had not thought of him for years but the name Jeff seemed to fit it.   Later I recalled his right name.

M: An elderly lady is here.   Her name begins with an R or a B.

Sitter: The younger lady's name began with a B.

M: Yes that is so.   It is the younger lady.   She didn't want to pass out.   You have been doing something for her. She thanks you and Jim.

(*Note:* An R and a B look much alike and the medium could easily have confused them if her visual imagery were not very clear.   The B suggested a young woman in the prime of life who did not want to pass out.   The little service that I had done her son did not occur to me to be worthy of thanks until the moment of this sitting.)

M: Did you come to investigate spirits?   I mean, to come near to spirits, some five, six or seven years ago?

Sitter: I nearly died.

M: Yes, that is it.

(*Note:* Some seven years before this séance I nearly died after an appendix operation.   In coming out of the ether I was much confused and the nurse appeared for the moment like a wraith.)

M: Is the elderly lady your mother?

Sitter: No, she was not my mother.

M: I put Henry in short pants ...... Did you have a relation who met with an accident which affected his neck? I can feel him going down, down, down.

Sitter: I had an uncle who was drowned.

M: He is with us.

(*Note:* I have no recollection of my first entrance into short pants, but I did have at that time an uncle who met with an accident at sea and was drowned. I do not remember whether he was injured before drowning.)

M: I get the name Bert. Does that mean anything to you?

Sitter: No.

M: Perhaps it is Albert.

Sitter: Yes, I know an Albert.

(*Note:* The elderly lady suggested was devoted to Albert. I often associate them together in my mind.)

M: An old sweetheart of yours is here. Her name begins with H.

Sitter: Could it be Helen?

M: Yes, that is it. She has put away the old things you gave her. You must read "Lavender and Old Lace" and you will understand.

(*Note:* I once knew a girl named Helen, though she was not a sweetheart. Perhaps when I read the book mentioned I will see some pertinent references. The young lady is associated with my first attendance at church.)

M: My guide says it seems as if you had been delayed in doing things you wanted to do, but in September or October you will enter into a new situation. You are going to get away from old conditions. Doors will be opened. There will be even a change in location. You have been released from old conditions. You are being helped by the young woman who recently passed out. One that is related to Jim. There is a spirit who passed out while taking ether. Do you know a Rodney or a Jacoby?

Sitter: No.

(*Note:* It is true that the following September found me in a new location far away from old conditions and engaged in a new occupation. I cannot recall a Rodney or Jacoby.)

M: Bessie is here. Sends love. Take care of yourself. I have not gone far from you. I am taking all the chances I can to pierce the veil. I will rap on the General; I mean his picture.

(*Note:* The name Bessie came in very promptly without any guessing whatever. It was the name of a cousin with whom I grew up in boyhood. The reference to the General is not clear. Occasionally I have been humorously called "General," though I did not believe that she knew of this.)

Sitter: We have no picture of a General, but sometimes I have been called "General."

M: Yes, she knows you were called "General."

(*Note:* During her lifetime she did not meet the people who called me General.)

M: She has a message for E. M. She says she has not forgotten what M has done for her and what she has done for B. M has brought up B. Says she knows what M is doing for B.

(*Note:* I have a cousin whom we call M. She has brought up her brother's child, whose name begins with B, from her early childhood to maturity.)

M: Name begins with P. I am also hearing an R and an A. Would it be Prather? Something went to the bottom with that name.

Sitter: That was the name of the uncle who was drowned, or rather the name sounded like that.

After these remarks the medium indulged in a little philosophy and some general statements about my work, which, with some statements about my health are not very interesting. The last statement she made ran as follows:

M: Guide says you are going to have many happy days in the body because you have not yet finished life's work. You are now going to begin to accomplish it, especially helped by one who went on before, the young lady who was B. She says "Little Boy Blue, you will understand."

(*Note:* There is no comment to make upon the Guide's prediction about the future. The reference to Little Boy Blue was quite a surprise. The morning before I went to the séance I dressed myself in a set of blue overalls and slipped on a blue coat to match. I happened to see myself in a large mirror and exclaimed, "Hello, Little Boy Blue with a bald head.")

In the foregoing report I have attempted to enter into the spirit of the situation very sympathetically. Everything the medium said I sought to find reflected in some experience during my life. Occasionally it called for some ingenuity to make connections. However it is quite evident that anyone who is thoroughly convinced that the message "coming through" has a bearing on his life and comes from someone who really knows his past will naturally find interpretations and explanations. In doing this his personal equation can work into his material so smoothly and easily that he is not even aware of the ingenuity he is putting forth to make sense out of the message.

Now let us turn to the same notes taken during the séance but studied in an entirely different mood. Instead of trying to find some meaning, obvious or hidden, in what was said, the attitude is to read what the message presented, think it over carefully and state frankly whether it has any application to the sitter's own life.

Sitting with Mrs. Sanders, July 27, 1926.

Mrs. Sanders seated herself in a large, comfortable chair and wrapped herself in several shawls. She placed a foot-stool with a cushion upon it at her feet, and covered her knees and feet with a large shawl. After a general conversation she placed a thick, blue bandage around her eyes and began to speak in the rôle of a medium.

M: I get the initial J. Also an L, a woman's name. She passed out three months ago.

(*Note:* No such woman known to me.)

M: The spirit of a gentleman is here. I see an old house among the trees, part of it is falling down. The word Illinois comes to me.

(*Note:* Am absolutely unacquainted with any houses in Illinois.)

M: Also an H. A spirit of a lady, motherly, not dead long. Abdominal trouble. She comes close to me. Her name begins with Em or M. Is perhaps forty or forty-five. Has dark hair, parted in the middle. Had three daughters. One daughter's name begins with M, the other one with P. She asks how A or J are.

(*Note:* I am unable to remember anyone who would fit in with the above description.)

M: Two parts of the family lived together while this lady was living.

(*Note:* Not being able to identify the woman, cannot say anything of her family.)

M: Is there a Jim?

Sitter: Yes, there is a Jim.

M: How is Jim? Sends her love to him. There has been some trouble three months ago. Something was sold. Did C have anything to do with it? I seem to get a C. Is it a C?

Sitter: No, it is an O.

M: Yes, that is right. It is an O.

(*Note:* A piece of property was sold about three months ago by a member of my family whose name began with an O. I suggested O. There was no "trouble." Simply a delay in making the sale.)

M: A man passed out near the old house. The name was W. He was probably shot. I get a Robert, Robert B. Or is it Robert C? Watkins, Wadley? No, it doesn't come quite clear. He calls you Henry.

(*Note:* The name Henry is correct, but I know of no one named Robert who was shot and killed. Also my boyhood friends never called me "Henry."

M: Are there five in the family?

Sitter: No, four.

M: Are you the last?

Sitter: No, third.

M: Don't they call you Doctor?

Sitter: Yes.

(*Note:* This may have been had over the phone.)

M: There seems to be a woman who might also be called Doctor. She is with you. She is very close to you. Don't know whether you are an M.D. or a D.D. Would her name be M? Also her name sounds like Laura.

(*Note:* I am not a D.D. or an M.D. I know of no woman doctor whose name begins with M or sounds like Laura.)

M: I find you three months ago having trouble. Something has to be cancelled. She calls "Hebe." She has crimpy hair. Gray blue eyes. Has very little hair.

(*Note:* I never knew a "Hebe.")

M: I am speaking of a young woman who is with her. She died of a fever, due to an accident. Her name is S or B. Weren't you near death in October or August?

Sitter: Yes, in October, some years ago.

(*Note:* I know of no one who died of fever after an accident.)

M: You have a brother who is a doctor. No? Oh, it's

a close friend, name begins with a T or an F.   He has a relation
in the spirit land.

(*Note:* When I told her my brother was not a doctor she
promptly substituted a friend and then made the broad statement that he had a relation in the spirit land. I have no
close friend whose name begins with a T or an F and who is
also a doctor.)

M: Bob says tell you Jeff is with him.

Sitter laughs.

M: Do you recognize Jeff?

Sitter: I wonder.   Isn't he a colored man?

M: Yes, that is it.   He is a colored man.

Sitter: Did he die of drink?

M: Yes, that is Jeff.

(*Note:* All through this it is quite obvious that the medium
is following the sitter's leads.)

M: An elderly lady is here.   Her name begins with an R
or a B.

Sitter: The younger lady's name began with a B.

M: Yes, that is so.   It is the younger lady.   She didn't
want to pass out.   You have been doing something for her.
She thanks you and Jim.

(*Note:* Again the medium followed my lead.   Her statements
had no significance.)

M: Did you come to investigate spirits?   I mean, to come
near to spirits, some five, six or seven years ago?

Sitter: I nearly died.

M: Yes, that's it.

(*Note:* Again the medium makes her message fit my explanation.)

M: Is the elderly lady your mother?

Sitter: No, she was not my mother.

M: I put Henry in short pants. . . . . Did you have a relation who met with an accident which affected his neck?   I
can feel him going down, down, down.

Sitter: I had an uncle who was drowned.

M: He is with us.

(*Note:* All of this is without any significance whatever.)

M: I get the name Bert. Does that mean anything to you?

Sitter: No.

M: Perhaps it is Albert.

Sitter: Yes, I know an Albert.

M: An old sweetheart of yours is here. Her name begins with H.

Sitter: Could it be "Helen?"

M: Yes, that is it. She has put away the old things that you gave her. You must read "Lavender and Old Lace" and you will understand.

(*Note:* Unable to locate any sweetheart named "Helen.")

M: My guide says it seems as if you had been delayed in doing things you wanted to do, but in September or October you will enter into a new situation. You are going to get away from old conditions. Doors will be opened. There will be even a change in location. You have been released from old conditions. You are being helped by the young woman who recently passed out. One that is related to Jim. There is a spirit who passed out while taking ether. Do you know a Rodney, or Jacoby?

Sitter: No.

M: Bessie is here. Sends love. Take care of yourself. I have not gone far from you. I am taking all the chances I can to pierce the veil. I will rap on the General; I mean his picture.

(*Note:* Had a cousin named Bessie who died four years ago. We were not very close. The reference to the general is unintelligible.)

Sitter: We have no picture of a general, but sometimes I have been called "General."

M: Yes, she knows you were called "General."

(*Note:* This is most improbable.)

M: She has a message for E. M. She says she has not forgotten what M has done for her, and what she has done for
B. M has brought up B. Says she knows what M is doing
for B.

(*Note:* I have a cousin M who, with others, has brought up a
child B. But Bessie knew nothing of this side of my family.)

M: Name begins with P. Am also hearing an R and an A.
Would it be Prather? Something went to the bottom with
that name.

Sitter: That was the name of the uncle who was drowned.
or rather the name sounded like that.

After these remarks the medium rambled off into
some broad general statements about life and advice
to me about my health none of which was significant.
Her last statement was:

M: Guide says you are going to have many happy days in
the body because you have not yet finished life's work. You
are now going to begin to accomplish it, especially helped by
one who went on before, the young lady who was B. She says,
"Little Boy Blue, you will understand."

(*Note:* The one thing in this statement which could have been
significant was the association of the young lady B and Little
Boy Blue. If the lady had ever called my attention to Little
Boy Blue either in pictures or poetry there might have been a
significance. As a matter of fact the lady was not young when
she died, she was about forty-five years of age and I had seen
little or nothing of her for some twenty-five years.)

Surely there is a very marked difference between
these two types of report. If you are interested in
following up the argument of this chapter, get Vol.

18 of the "Proceedings of the American Society for Psychical Research." In it you will find an account of the same Mrs. Sanders having five sittings in which everything said by the medium and sitter is carefully recorded. Notice that it is edited by W. F. Prince, Ph.D. of the American Society for Psychical Research. Judge for yourself what his personal equation was.

CHAPTER XI

WHY WE ARE SUPERSTITIOUS

NEW YORK'S famous sky-line expresses more than the wealth and genius of a young nation. It is the expression of a great body of knowledge. Each of those towering buildings is made possible by modern science. Years of inconspicuous labor in hundreds of laboratories by a great number of men evolved the ideas that are built into those structures. A fairly good measure of the knowledge of a people is to be found in the things they build. Between a canoe moored by a Brazilian Indian village and the Mauretania in New York lie centuries of acquired information.

In gradually building up the mass of knowledge that comprises science, the hardest and slowest part was in the beginnings. Once the right methods were found and some instruments devised to help in making observations it would seem that the sciences grew with astonishing rapidity. Most of the inertia in getting started lay in the peculiar difficulty of forming new habits in thinking. For the sort of knowledge that constitutes the civilized man's equipment calls for an attitude that seems most unnatural to simpler people. Indeed, the very common ideas of

178

mathematical accuracy, careful observations, critical deductions are simply not known among the primitive people and it calls for long and exacting training for them to take up the scientists' method of acquiring knowledge.

Indeed, the way of getting information as well as the character of the information is so different between the men "in a state of nature" and the men who live in our artificial civilization that it is quite worth our while to note these differences. Especially is this worthy of attention, because a very great number of our citizens are not trained scientists and they mix primitive thinking with their modern thinking.

One of the chief sources of knowledge among primitive people is *authority*. A few old men or women have the knowledge which has come down to them from the years. Their statements carry great weight. If they have the intelligence to give some valuable decisions, their prestige becomes enormous. Knowledge gained in this way is very congenial to the average human being. He learns to accept his elders' ideas in his childhood and the habit of taking ready made conceptions is hard to abandon later. All through the Middle Ages the thinking world preferred to take Aristotle's statements rather than to experiment and learn for themselves. Today a very large percent of our people accept opinions from any well-advertised source. Often an argument is settled and an opponent squashed by an apt quotation from some well-known man.   A great many people believe in spiritualism because of Oliver Lodge and Conan Doyle.   An "authority" is a lazy or ignorant man's best friend.

Another trait that characterizes both primitive men and children is the *mixing of emotion into the thinking* that supplies their information.   An unfriendly tribe is hated, therefore they are known as inferiors or monsters.   Dangerous animals are known to have mystic powers.   Children know queer things about dark cellars and thunder storms at night.   We have just passed through an acrimonious era.   Prohibition advocates have painted pictures of their opponents that were based on a hatred of excessive drinking.   Their antagonists developed a propaganda conveying the idea that all prohibitionists were joyless, overbearing, and victims of one idea.   These are rather obvious examples of emotional thinking.   As a matter of fact, very little thinking is free from some form of emotion.   Among thinking people who are careful of their product there is always a caution against allowing the emotions to enter.   Two men translating the same Latin author have produced strikingly different results according to their feelings concerning the odes they interpreted.   Two scientists measuring a bar of aluminum got results quite unlike because one had a strong feeling that his previous records showed too short readings.   Very subtly one's feelings weave their way into his thinking and give it a direction that is due to the emotional tone. Of course there are many obvious examples of people who frankly allow their feelings to form their convictions. Quite sensible young men have solemnly informed me that they believed in the freedom of the will because life wouldn't be worth living if they considered themselves the result of the interplay of physical and mental laws. Almost any good Christian Scientist will tell you that she has embraced Mrs. Eddy's doctrine because it makes her so happy. Not a few of the thorough-going spiritualists admit that their beliefs conform with their wishes, and that life would be a sorry affair if they could not anticipate immortality.

Primitive people and civilized adults do a great deal of *group thinking*. By that I mean they conform with the ideas of a group and willingly defend them. Such convictions are often handed down from generation to generation. They become firmly fixed. Only the most hardy thinker dare set his ideas up against the common belief. Seemingly, human nature is so constructed it unwillingly admits changes in convictions.

When a group of beliefs have become identified with an organization, they acquire a great strength. Rivalry with other organizations sharpens a belief which is loyally defended. Science has for centuries combated the beliefs of the organized churches. In some instances science supplied concepts of greater

dignity and beauty than those the church held, but
the church fought vigorously against them. A reason
for this is to be found in the way that each man or-
ganizes his ideas about the values of life. When a
man has satisfied himself that his life is a school and
preparation for a future life and has acquired habits
of feeling and acting in accordance with that conviction, it is clearly a personal disaster for him to abandon such a belief. Here is the reason why men cannot change their thinking to conform with ideas that
are more logical than those they have been holding.

Again the primitive mind makes its appearance in
our present day, by following *simple forms of reason-
ing*. Among men who have not had the benefit of
a thorough education and who possess simply an
average intelligence it is common to find them arguing
from one or two instances to a general conclusion.
Recently I heard a farmer maintain that hunting
dogs could not catch the scent of quail more than fifteen feet away. This conviction arose from the fact
that our dogs missed a couple of coveys by about
twenty feet. Fishermen are full of stout beliefs that
certain fish do certain things and defend their statements with two or three examples. Every political
campaign supplies us with politicians who clinch
their arguments by citing a single case chosen from
history. Obviously this sort of thinking has nothing
in common with science. Since the time of Roger
Bacon, we have had the laws of induction clearly

before us. It is one of the characteristics of modern science that no general conclusion can be drawn while contradictory facts may be collected. Only tentative laws may be established in many cases. One of the best illustrations of scientific attack upon a problem is afforded by Jenner before the time that our modern science had established its methods. Jenner cited so many cases where cow-pox made its victims immune to small-pox that neither the skeptical physicians nor the hostile churches could deny him. Indeed, if any one thing characterizes our modern science it is this insistence upon a large number of observations to establish any generalization. For some years psychologists have made a practise of reporting the number of cases they use in their experiments and they show mathematically how the possibility of chance diminishes as they increase the number of cases studied. Psychic research has been deplorably faulty in the reports it has made in defense of the principles it has claimed.

It is so easy to draw conclusions from *simple analogies* that we find everyone doing it. With primitive people it is very quaint and amusing. Loud noises frighten away dangerous animals and sneak thieves at night, therefore the evil spirit that rustles the leaves by your window may be frightened away by a loud shout. Fearful odors will drive anyone away. For that reason the sick savage sometimes covers his body with filth to drive the sick demon into other

quarters. Before we began to study the chemical
action of drugs upon the tissues of the body our ancestors hit upon some analogies. If there was trouble
with the blood they used blood-root on account of
its red juice; if the liver made trouble they used liver-
wort as it has a leaf shaped like the liver; eye-bright
with a spot like an eye was good for eye troubles;
bear grease coming from an animal with thick hair
was entrusted with the duty of growing hair on bald
heads. Since the radio has appeared, we find thou-
sands of people believing in telepathy. A few instances where two people entertained the same
thoughts at the same time is interpreted as a principle
that one mind can affect another by thought-waves.
Since radio sending and receiving sets may be sta-
tioned far apart and one mind communicate with
another by way of ether waves, it is plain that the
electricity in the nerve currents of one brain may
start an ether agitation which will cause the currents
in another brain to stir up like thoughts! To anyone who has dissected a brain this analogy is simply
maddening.

All through the thinking of primitive people and
little children runs a characteristic trait. In the
study of tribal beliefs the world over *animism* stands
out prominently. The minds of both children and
savages work in the same ways for the same reasons.
Children come into a world made up of things and
other people. Long before they adjust themselves

to things and understand them, they have learned to
adjust themselves to people. A baby of eighteen
months knows a very great deal about people. It
distinguishes between pleasant mothers and unpleas-
ant nurses, boisterous fathers and diffident strangers.
Not a little shrewd understanding of human nature
may be seen in these little folk. After they have
fairly well acquainted themselves with human nature
they undertake the difficult task of adjusting themselves to the myriad of things about them. From
their first training in adjusting themselves to human
nature they carry over habits into their management
of inanimate things. This is the explanation of a
child's behavior when the wheels of his toy stick and
he hits it and cries. This is why children endow dead
things with lively feelings. It is natural to them to
explain the moving cloud as a living thing, to think
of thunder and lightning as the expression of anger
by some feeling agent. This is a trait that easily
becomes fixed. All through life, not a few people
find themselves slipping back into this child habit.
A famous psychologist was caught in San Francisco
during the earthquake and fire. He ran out into the
streets and tried to escape the flames and falling walls.
Every way he turned some danger sprang up to face
him. So baffling did this become that it seemed to
him that there was a purpose in it. He found himself thinking of the natural processes of combustion
and gravity in terms of a personality. Something

monstrous and vicious with evil design seemed to him to actuate the dangers around him. Another scientist swimming in the ocean was caught by the undertow. Swim as he would he slowly drifted out to sea. He found that he gained shoreward if he put forth his best efforts as the waves swept by him. Soon it became a sort of combat between the swimmer and the surf. Eventually a large wave hurled him upon the beach. Slowly he rose and made a face at the sea. In private he admitted that he had felt as though the water were an antagonist. When the struggle was over he had won over a vicious opponent. This feeling was so strong that he didn't resist the temptation to express his triumph. Everyday commonplace experiences bring out the same traits in the ordinary citizen. He gets angry when the lawn-mower jams, he kicks angrily when his self-starter won't work, and he blames his luck as a pagan would blame his god, when his horse loses the race. Probably no human being ever loses this childish habit.

Books have been written upon animism as it appears among simple people. The term is derived from the Latin *animus*, meaning "thought", "feeling", "life". Inanimate things are animate among savages. Naturally this must be so, for what they know best has to do with human purposes, ideas, and emotions. When they are provoked they slash out and smash what opposes them, when they are hungry and thirsty they fight vigorously for relief. Their tenderest emotions lead them to care for their offspring. All of these forces in human nature are thoroughly familiar to them. Forces that flash thunder-bolts into trees, forces that raise ominous clouds and terrific storms, forces that gently shelter the hanging fruit with shady leaves are all totally unknown to them. What explanation can they give for the activities of nature all around them? Quite obviously they must make their interpretations in terms of what they feel that they understand. This leads them to endow the objects around them with natures somewhat like their own.

Sharply contrasted with the sort of knowledge that primitive people gather is the knowledge that modern science has acquired. The outstanding distinction between these two types is that modern science uncovers a principle of orderliness in the universe, whereas the pre-scientific notions had a medley of principles. Each stride forward that science makes lays bare the connections which apparently separated phenomena. Recently we have seen how the very fine rays of ether forming the X-ray unite with the great broadcasting waves of the radio. Each year gives us a new insight into the secrets of nature. The atom is slowly giving up its secrets. Twenty-five hundred years ago, shrewd Greek thinkers claimed that matter could be separated into atoms. Their brilliant genius never envisaged the marvelous table

of atoms that our school boys know. Starting with
a simple element like hydrogen he learns that there is
a proton around which an electron circles; the next
element, helium, has one proton and two electrons.
Ninety-two elements fall into their places with beautiful precision as their protons and electrons form
different configurations. Search the universe where
we will and these two great natural and simple arrangements of waves and atoms are present. Conceptions of such beauty and grandeur were impossible
to men who interpreted the universe about them
piece-meal. Indeed, the trained scientist never looks
for sharp or abrupt changes in the principles that
underlie nature. All of his experiences lead him to
expect that the uniformities he has been finding will
continue into whatever realms he explores. This
striking contrast between the conceptions of the
modern trained mind and those of the primitive man
(and the inadequately educated) resembles the difference between the methods of acquiring knowledge
before the time of Francis Bacon and those of our
day. Bacon became disgusted with the haphazard
way of trying to build up information about nature
in ways that were illustrative of all the traits of childish thinking that we have just noted. He insisted
that the only way to amass knowledge was by col-
lecting a great mass of facts. Let the facts be what
they may, man's only obligation is to assemble them.
After he has a vast number of them then he may

arrange them in various ways to discover whether
there is any principle or law that relates them. Of
course this is an ideal procedure. As a matter of
fact scientists usually make a guess concerning some
principle in nature and then search for facts to sup-
port it or to reject it. Always the *fact* is the deciding
matter. That means good observations. Faulty
observation means distorted facts. Not a little of
the marvelous advance in recent years is due to im-
provement in observation. The microscope, telescope and photography have been enormous aids.
But apart from these the insistence by scientists upon
many observations and especially controlled observations have made for dependable knowledge. Thus
an Austrian monk hits upon a principle in nature
which shows that, by cross-breeding high-growing and
low-growing garden peas, their offspring will appear
with certain characteristics through a number of
generations. After a great number of experiments
and careful observations it was learned that this
principle applies not simply to plants but also to
animals. However, when we attempt to discover its
application to human beings, we cannot make such
accurate observations. We cannot experimentally
mate two people, acquire a lot of offspring and mate
them. Only as we make our observation under good
or controlled conditions can we hope for certainty.

Contrast the habit of thinking of the trained scientific mind and his methods of studying nature with

the haphazard hit and miss ways of the average citizen. All of the superstitions that characterize our fellow-men grow up because of the natural propensity to think as men did before the time of Bacon. A belief still persists with many uneducated people that the moon has a great influence over the weather. It is supposed that the new, full, and half moon may bring about such changes. Not one of these believers has even kept a true and faithful record of changes in the moon and the weather to see whether they tally. Throughout many sections of the country the people will gather to pray for rain after a long drought. Even the most courageous will often pray for protection in a violent thunderstorm. Here is the old principle of animism, assuming a vague kind of mind controlling precipitation and electricity. As for superstitions concerning the sex of the unborn child, they are legion. Slowly the superstition that the thoughts and feelings of the mother will influence the nature of her unborn child is disappearing. This is because of discoveries in embryology. It is not due to any careful observation on the part of parents to discover whether such practices are practical. From time immemorial men who raised crops have appealed to their gods, demons, spirits and saints, because so many chances controlled the growth in their fields.

Luck is a mysterious thing. Nearly every average citizen believes in luck. He has no clear notion of just what luck is but in the back of his mind there is a vague idea that luck is not simply chance. If he is a firm believer in luck he will often have notions as to how it works. He can cite instances of certain days or numbers that have a peculiar significance for him. Possibly he has a lucky stone or coin or curio which he feels he must carry with him. This is just one step above the animism of the savage with his amulet. It may be exaggerating the notion of luck to claim that it is animistic. With many people, certainly, their conception of luck involves the idea of some mystic plan or purpose.

We find the ordinary individual who has not had high-school training and who is utterly unacquainted with the habits of thinking that characterize the trained scientific mind very prone to explain matters he cannot understand in the simple ways of the primitive man or the child. Perhaps we should not limit this observation to the uneducated as I have met a number of college graduates who lapse into the same sort of natural superstitions. For example I recall a highly educated and very talented lady who did automatic writing. I have seen her hand quickly cover a page with perfectly intelligent sentences while she was engaged in an animated conversation which had nothing to do with which she was writing. She tried to fight off the notion that her hand was controlled by an independent spirit. As she had no explanation for the curious behavior of her hand and as it seemed to move quite independently of her will she was disposed to lapse into the type of thinking which characterizes animism. Another educated young lady saw a vivid appearance of her dead husband and knowing no explanation concluded that it was an apparition. Many people hear voices speaking to them and will dimly glimpse vague faces looking at them when they are entirely alone. Commonly they make their explanation in terms of primitive thinking. Perhaps it is too much to expect them to attempt experiments and to study the conditions under which these things occur.

It is rather disappointing to an educator in this twentieth century to find a great number of people who abandon the sort of mental habits they were taught and who lapse into childish thinking, when they receive some surprising message from a medium. Time and again I meet such people who have had some insight into scientific methods but who make no effort to apply them. One or two striking experiences are sufficient for them. Indeed, the disposition to lapse into superstition is so strong that almost anything that is a little difficult to relate to familiar things brings out the pre-scientific types of thinking.

Naturally then we must expect to find a very great number of people who are easily convinced of the claims of spiritualism. It would seem that the natural propensity to think as human beings have thought for fifty-thousand years easily over-rides the acquired methods of the last few centuries.